TABLE OF CONTENTS

Copyright © Mometrix Media. You have been licensed one copy of this document for personal use only. Any other reproduction or redistribution is strictly prohibited. All rights reserved.

Secret Key #1 - Time is Your Greatest Enemy

Pace Yourself

Wear a watch. At the beginning of the test, check the time (or start a chronometer on your watch to count the minutes), and check the time after every few questions to make sure you are "on schedule."

If you are forced to speed up, do it efficiently. Usually one or more answer choices can be eliminated without too much difficulty. Above all, don't panic. Don't speed up and just begin guessing at random choices. By pacing yourself, and continually monitoring your progress against your watch, you will always know exactly how far ahead or behind you are with your available time. If you find that you are one minute behind on the test, don't skip one question without spending any time on it, just to catch back up. Take 15 fewer seconds on the next four questions, and after four questions you'll have caught back up. Once you catch back up, you can continue working each problem at your normal pace.

Furthermore, don't dwell on the problems that you were rushed on. If a problem was taking up too much time and you made a hurried guess, it must be difficult. The difficult questions are the ones you are most likely to miss anyway, so it isn't a big loss. It is better to end with more time than you need than to run out of time.

Lastly, sometimes it is beneficial to slow down if you are constantly getting ahead of time. You are always more likely to catch a careless mistake by working more slowly than quickly, and among very high-scoring test takers (those who are likely to have lots of time left over), careless errors affect the score more than mastery of material.

Copyright © Mometrix Media. You have been licensed one copy of this document for personal use only.
Any other reproduction or redistribution is strictly prohibited. All rights reserved.

Secret Key #2 - Guessing is not Guesswork

You probably know that guessing is a good idea - unlike other standardized tests, there is no penalty for getting a wrong answer. Even if you have no idea about a question, you still have a 20-25% chance of getting it right.

Most test takers do not understand the impact that proper guessing can have on their score. Unless you score extremely high, guessing will significantly contribute to your final score.

Monkeys Take the Test

What most test takers don't realize is that to insure that 20-25% chance, you have to guess randomly. If you put 20 monkeys in a room to take this test, assuming they answered once per question and behaved themselves, on average they would get 20-25% of the questions correct. Put 20 test takers in the room, and the average will be much lower among guessed questions. Why?

1. The test writers intentionally writes deceptive answer choices that "look" right. A test taker has no idea about a question, so picks the "best looking" answer, which is often wrong. The monkey has no idea what looks good and what doesn't, so will consistently be lucky about 20-25% of the time.
2. Test takers will eliminate answer choices from the guessing pool based on a hunch or intuition. Simple but correct answers often get excluded, leaving a 0% chance of being correct. The monkey has no clue, and often gets lucky with the best choice.

This is why the process of elimination endorsed by most test courses is flawed and detrimental to your performance- test takers don't guess, they make an ignorant stab in the dark that is usually worse than random.

$5 Challenge

Let me introduce one of the most valuable ideas of this course- the $5 challenge:

You only mark your "best guess" if you are willing to bet $5 on it.
You only eliminate choices from guessing if you are willing to bet $5 on it.

Why $5? Five dollars is an amount of money that is small yet not insignificant, and can really add up fast (20 questions could cost you $100). Likewise, each answer choice on one question of the test will have a small impact on your overall score, but it can really add up to a lot of points in the end.

Copyright © Mometrix Media. You have been licensed one copy of this document for personal use only.
Any other reproduction or redistribution is strictly prohibited. All rights reserved.

The process of elimination IS valuable. The following shows your chance of guessing it right:

If you eliminate wrong answer choices until only this many remain:	1	2	3
Chance of getting it correct:	100%	50%	33%

However, if you accidentally eliminate the right answer or go on a hunch for an incorrect answer, your chances drop dramatically: to 0%. By guessing among all the answer choices, you are GUARANTEED to have a shot at the right answer.

That's why the $5 test is so valuable- if you give up the advantage and safety of a pure guess, it had better be worth the risk.

What we still haven't covered is how to be sure that whatever guess you make is truly random. Here's the easiest way:

Always pick the first answer choice among those remaining.

Such a technique means that you have decided, **before you see a single test question**, exactly how you are going to guess- and since the order of choices tells you nothing about which one is correct, this guessing technique is perfectly random.

This section is not meant to scare you away from making educated guesses or eliminating choices- you just need to define when a choice is worth eliminating. The $5 test, along with a pre-defined random guessing strategy, is the best way to make sure you reap all of the benefits of guessing.

*Copyright © Mometrix Media. You have been licensed one copy of this document for personal use only.
Any other reproduction or redistribution is strictly prohibited. All rights reserved.*

Secret Key #3 - Practice Smarter, Not Harder

Many test takers delay the test preparation process because they dread the awful amounts of practice time they think necessary to succeed on the test. We have refined an effective method that will take you only a fraction of the time.

There are a number of "obstacles" in your way to succeed. Among these are answering questions, finishing in time, and mastering test-taking strategies. All must be executed on the day of the test at peak performance, or your score will suffer. The test is a mental marathon that has a large impact on your future.

Just like a marathon runner, it is important to work your way up to the full challenge. So first you just worry about questions, and then time, and finally strategy:

Success Strategy

1. Find a good source for practice tests.
2. If you are willing to make a larger time investment, consider using more than one study guide- often the different approaches of multiple authors will help you "get" difficult concepts.
3. Take a practice test with no time constraints, with all study helps "open book." Take your time with questions and focus on applying strategies.
4. Take a practice test with time constraints, with all guides "open book."
5. Take a final practice test with no open material and time limits

If you have time to take more practice tests, just repeat step 5. By gradually exposing yourself to the full rigors of the test environment, you will condition your mind to the stress of test day and maximize your success.

Copyright © Mometrix Media. You have been licensed one copy of this document for personal use only. Any other reproduction or redistribution is strictly prohibited. All rights reserved.

Secret Key #4 - Prepare, Don't Procrastinate

Let me state an obvious fact: if you take the test three times, you will get three different scores. This is due to the way you feel on test day, the level of preparedness you have, and, despite the test writers' claims to the contrary, some tests WILL be easier for you than others.

Since your future depends so much on your score, you should maximize your chances of success. In order to maximize the likelihood of success, you've got to prepare in advance. This means taking practice tests and spending time learning the information and test taking strategies you will need to succeed.

Never take the test as a "practice" test, expecting that you can just take it again if you need to. Feel free to take sample tests on your own, but when you go to take the official test, be prepared, be focused, and do your best the first time!

Copyright © Mometrix Media. You have been licensed one copy of this document for personal use only. Any other reproduction or redistribution is strictly prohibited. All rights reserved.

Secret Key #5 - Test Yourself

Everyone knows that time is money. There is no need to spend too much of your time or too little of your time preparing for the test. You should only spend as much of your precious time preparing as is necessary for you to get the score you need.

Once you have taken a practice test under real conditions of time constraints, then you will know if you are ready for the test or not.

If you have scored extremely high the first time that you take the practice test, then there is not much point in spending countless hours studying. You are already there.

Benchmark your abilities by retaking practice tests and seeing how much you have improved. Once you score high enough to guarantee success, then you are ready.

If you have scored well below where you need, then knuckle down and begin studying in earnest. Check your improvement regularly through the use of practice tests under real conditions. Above all, don't worry, panic, or give up. The key is perseverance!

Then, when you go to take the test, remain confident and remember how well you did on the practice tests. If you can score high enough on a practice test, then you can do the same on the real thing.

Copyright © Mometrix Media. You have been licensed one copy of this document for personal use only. Any other reproduction or redistribution is strictly prohibited. All rights reserved.

General Strategies

The most important thing you can do is to ignore your fears and jump into the test immediately- do not be overwhelmed by any strange-sounding terms. You have to jump into the test like jumping into a pool- all at once is the easiest way.

Make Predictions

As you read and understand the question, try to guess what the answer will be. Remember that several of the answer choices are wrong, and once you begin reading them, your mind will immediately become cluttered with answer choices designed to throw you off. Your mind is typically the most focused immediately after you have read the question and digested its contents. If you can, try to predict what the correct answer will be. You may be surprised at what you can predict.

Quickly scan the choices and see if your prediction is in the listed answer choices. If it is, then you can be quite confident that you have the right answer. It still won't hurt to check the other answer choices, but most of the time, you've got it!

Answer the Question

It may seem obvious to only pick answer choices that answer the question, but the test writers can create some excellent answer choices that are wrong. Don't pick an answer just because it sounds right, or you believe it to be true. It MUST answer the question. Once you've made your selection, always go back and check it against the question and make sure that you didn't misread the question, and the answer choice does answer the question posed.

Benchmark

After you read the first answer choice, decide if you think it sounds correct or not. If it doesn't, move on to the next answer choice. If it does, mentally mark that answer choice. This doesn't mean that you've definitely selected it as your answer choice, it just means that it's the best you've seen thus far. Go ahead and read the next choice. If the next choice is worse than the one you've already selected, keep going to the next answer choice. If the next choice is better than the choice you've already selected, mentally mark the new answer choice as your best guess.

The first answer choice that you select becomes your standard. Every other answer choice must be benchmarked against that standard. That choice is correct until proven otherwise by another answer choice beating it out. Once you've decided that no other answer choice seems as good, do one final check to ensure that your answer choice answers the question posed.

Valid Information

Don't discount any of the information provided in the question. Every piece of information may be necessary to determine the correct answer. None of the information in the question is there to throw you off (while the answer choices will certainly have information to throw you off). If two seemingly unrelated topics are discussed, don't ignore either. You can be confident there is a relationship, or it wouldn't be included in the question, and you are probably going to have to determine what is that relationship to find the answer.

Copyright © Mometrix Media. You have been licensed one copy of this document for personal use only. Any other reproduction or redistribution is strictly prohibited. All rights reserved.

Avoid "Fact Traps"

Don't get distracted by a choice that is factually true. Your search is for the answer that answers the question. Stay focused and don't fall for an answer that is true but incorrect. Always go back to the question and make sure you're choosing an answer that actually answers the question and is not just a true statement. An answer can be factually correct, but it MUST answer the question asked. Additionally, two answers can both be seemingly correct, so be sure to read all of the answer choices, and make sure that you get the one that BEST answers the question.

Milk the Question

Some of the questions may throw you completely off. They might deal with a subject you have not been exposed to, or one that you haven't reviewed in years. While your lack of knowledge about the subject will be a hindrance, the question itself can give you many clues that will help you find the correct answer. Read the question carefully and look for clues. Watch particularly for adjectives and nouns describing difficult terms or words that you don't recognize. Regardless of if you completely understand a word or not, replacing it with a synonym either provided or one you more familiar with may help you to understand what the questions are asking. Rather than wracking your mind about specific detailed information concerning a difficult term or word, try to use mental substitutes that are easier to understand.

The Trap of Familiarity

Don't just choose a word because you recognize it. On difficult questions, you may not recognize a number of words in the answer choices. The test writers don't put "make-believe" words on the test; so don't think that just because you only recognize all the words in one answer choice means that answer choice must be correct. If you only recognize words in one answer choice, then focus on that one. Is it correct? Try your best to determine if it is correct. If it is, that is great, but if it doesn't, eliminate it. Each word and answer choice you eliminate increases your chances of getting the question correct, even if you then have to guess among the unfamiliar choices.

Eliminate Answers

Eliminate choices as soon as you realize they are wrong. But be careful! Make sure you consider all of the possible answer choices. Just because one appears right, doesn't mean that the next one won't be even better! The test writers will usually put more than one good answer choice for every question, so read all of them. Don't worry if you are stuck between two that seem right. By getting down to just two remaining possible choices, your odds are now 50/50. Rather than wasting too much time, play the odds. You are guessing, but guessing wisely, because you've been able to knock out some of the answer choices that you know are wrong. If you are eliminating choices and realize that the last answer choice you are left with is also obviously wrong, don't panic. Start over and consider each choice again. There may easily be something that you missed the first time and will realize on the second pass.

Tough Questions

If you are stumped on a problem or it appears too hard or too difficult, don't waste time. Move on! Remember though, if you can quickly check for obviously incorrect answer choices, your chances of guessing correctly are greatly improved. Before you completely give up, at least try to knock out a couple of possible answers. Eliminate what you can and then guess at the remaining answer choices before moving on.

Copyright © Mometrix Media. You have been licensed one copy of this document for personal use only. Any other reproduction or redistribution is strictly prohibited. All rights reserved.

Brainstorm

If you get stuck on a difficult question, spend a few seconds quickly brainstorming. Run through the complete list of possible answer choices. Look at each choice and ask yourself, "Could this answer the question satisfactorily?" Go through each answer choice and consider it independently of the other. By systematically going through all possibilities, you may find something that you would otherwise overlook. Remember that when you get stuck, it's important to try to keep moving.

Read Carefully

Understand the problem. Read the question and answer choices carefully. Don't miss the question because you misread the terms. You have plenty of time to read each question thoroughly and make sure you understand what is being asked. Yet a happy medium must be attained, so don't waste too much time. You must read carefully, but efficiently.

Face Value

When in doubt, use common sense. Always accept the situation in the problem at face value. Don't read too much into it. These problems will not require you to make huge leaps of logic. The test writers aren't trying to throw you off with a cheap trick. If you have to go beyond creativity and make a leap of logic in order to have an answer choice answer the question, then you should look at the other answer choices. Don't overcomplicate the problem by creating theoretical relationships or explanations that will warp time or space. These are normal problems rooted in reality. It's just that the applicable relationship or explanation may not be readily apparent and you have to figure things out. Use your common sense to interpret anything that isn't clear.

Prefixes

If you're having trouble with a word in the question or answer choices, try dissecting it. Take advantage of every clue that the word might include. Prefixes and suffixes can be a huge help. Usually they allow you to determine a basic meaning. Pre- means before, post- means after, pro - is positive, de- is negative. From these prefixes and suffixes, you can get an idea of the general meaning of the word and try to put it into context. Beware though of any traps. Just because con is the opposite of pro, doesn't necessarily mean congress is the opposite of progress!

Hedge Phrases

Watch out for critical "hedge" phrases, such as likely, may, can, will often, sometimes, often, almost, mostly, usually, generally, rarely, sometimes. Question writers insert these hedge phrases to cover every possibility. Often an answer choice will be wrong simply because it leaves no room for exception. Avoid answer choices that have definitive words like "exactly," and "always".

Switchback Words

Stay alert for "switchbacks". These are the words and phrases frequently used to alert you to shifts in thought. The most common switchback word is "but". Others include although, however, nevertheless, on the other hand, even though, while, in spite of, despite, regardless of.

New Information

Correct answer choices will rarely have completely new information included. Answer choices typically are straightforward reflections of the material asked about and will directly relate to the question. If a new piece of information is included in an answer choice that doesn't even seem to relate to the topic being asked about, then that answer choice is likely incorrect. All of the

Copyright © Mometrix Media. You have been licensed one copy of this document for personal use only. Any other reproduction or redistribution is strictly prohibited. All rights reserved.

information needed to answer the question is usually provided for you, and so you should not have to make guesses that are unsupported or choose answer choices that require unknown information that cannot be reasoned on its own.

Time Management

On technical questions, don't get lost on the technical terms. Don't spend too much time on any one question. If you don't know what a term means, then since you don't have a dictionary, odds are you aren't going to get much further. You should immediately recognize terms as whether or not you know them. If you don't, work with the other clues that you have, the other answer choices and terms provided, but don't waste too much time trying to figure out a difficult term.

Contextual Clues

Look for contextual clues. An answer can be right but not correct. The contextual clues will help you find the answer that is most right and is correct. Understand the context in which a phrase or statement is made. This will help you make important distinctions.

Don't Panic

Panicking will not answer any questions for you. Therefore, it isn't helpful. When you first see the question, if your mind goes blank, take a deep breath. Force yourself to mechanically go through the steps of solving the problem and using the strategies you've learned.

Pace Yourself

Don't get clock fever. It's easy to be overwhelmed when you're looking at a page full of questions, your mind is full of random thoughts and feeling confused, and the clock is ticking down faster than you would like. Calm down and maintain the pace that you have set for yourself. As long as you are on track by monitoring your pace, you are guaranteed to have enough time for yourself. When you get to the last few minutes of the test, it may seem like you won't have enough time left, but if you only have as many questions as you should have left at that point, then you're right on track!

Answer Selection

The best way to pick an answer choice is to eliminate all of those that are wrong, until only one is left and confirm that is the correct answer. Sometimes though, an answer choice may immediately look right. Be careful! Take a second to make sure that the other choices are not equally obvious. Don't make a hasty mistake. There are only two times that you should stop before checking other answers. First is when you are positive that the answer choice you have selected is correct. Second is when time is almost out and you have to make a quick guess!

Check Your Work

Since you will probably not know every term listed and the answer to every question, it is important that you get credit for the ones that you do know. Don't miss any questions through careless mistakes. If at all possible, try to take a second to look back over your answer selection and make sure you've selected the correct answer choice and haven't made a costly careless mistake (such as marking an answer choice that you didn't mean to mark). This quick double check should more than pay for itself in caught mistakes for the time it costs.

Beware of Directly Quoted Answers

Sometimes an answer choice will repeat word for word a portion of the question or reference

Copyright © Mometrix Media. You have been licensed one copy of this document for personal use only. Any other reproduction or redistribution is strictly prohibited. All rights reserved.

section. However, beware of such exact duplication – it may be a trap! More than likely, the correct choice will paraphrase or summarize a point, rather than being exactly the same wording.

Slang

Scientific sounding answers are better than slang ones. An answer choice that begins "To compare the outcomes…" is much more likely to be correct than one that begins "Because some people insisted…"

Extreme Statements

Avoid wild answers that throw out highly controversial ideas that are proclaimed as established fact. An answer choice that states the "process should used in certain situations, if…" is much more likely to be correct than one that states the "process should be discontinued completely." The first is a calm rational statement and doesn't even make a definitive, uncompromising stance, using a hedge word "if" to provide wiggle room, whereas the second choice is a radical idea and far more extreme.

Answer Choice Families

When you have two or more answer choices that are direct opposites or parallels, one of them is usually the correct answer. For instance, if one answer choice states "x increases" and another answer choice states "x decreases" or "y increases," then those two or three answer choices are very similar in construction and fall into the same family of answer choices. A family of answer choices is when two or three answer choices are very similar in construction, and yet often have a directly opposite meaning. Usually the correct answer choice will be in that family of answer choices. The "odd man out" or answer choice that doesn't seem to fit the parallel construction of the other answer choices is more likely to be incorrect.

Copyright © Mometrix Media. You have been licensed one copy of this document for personal use only. Any other reproduction or redistribution is strictly prohibited. All rights reserved.

Top 20 Test Taking Tips

1. Carefully follow all the test registration procedures
2. Know the test directions, duration, topics, question types, how many questions
3. Setup a flexible study schedule at least 3-4 weeks before test day
4. Study during the time of day you are most alert, relaxed, and stress free
5. Maximize your learning style; visual learner use visual study aids, auditory learner use auditory study aids
6. Focus on your weakest knowledge base
7. Find a study partner to review with and help clarify questions
8. Practice, practice, practice
9. Get a good night's sleep; don't try to cram the night before the test
10. Eat a well balanced meal
11. Know the exact physical location of the testing site; drive the route to the site prior to test day
12. Bring a set of ear plugs; the testing center could be noisy
13. Wear comfortable, loose fitting, layered clothing to the testing center; prepare for it to be either cold or hot during the test
14. Bring at least 2 current forms of ID to the testing center
15. Arrive to the test early; be prepared to wait and be patient
16. Eliminate the obviously wrong answer choices, then guess the first remaining choice
17. Pace yourself; don't rush, but keep working and move on if you get stuck
18. Maintain a positive attitude even if the test is going poorly
19. Keep your first answer unless you are positive it is wrong
20. Check your work, don't make a careless mistake

Copyright © Mometrix Media. You have been licensed one copy of this document for personal use only. Any other reproduction or redistribution is strictly prohibited. All rights reserved.

Library Media Specialist

CD-ROM cost concerns

Five cost concerns in purchasing CD-ROMs for student instruction:
- CD-ROMs may be expensive but can be a cost-effective purchase if they are targeted upon curriculum objectives. Choosing appropriate CD-ROMs is a major concern of library media specialists.
- CD-ROM products may be widely advertised but little reviewed. The library media specialist should buy CD-ROM products which have been often tested and reviewed by classroom or library specialists.
- Structured search capability is a major concern in considering CD-ROM purchases.
- CD-ROM purchasing decisions must be tied to educational goals and objectives of the academic institution.
- Decisions must be made regarding the choice of full-text CD-ROMs or CD-ROM indexing sources. CD-ROM information products like EBSCO's magazine summaries combine sophisticated search capacities with the ability to transfer keyword searching experience to traditional periodical searches and online library catalogs.

Library media program goals

The AASL (American Association of School Libraries) has identified four important educational goals of a library media program:
- To provide access to information contained in an organized collection of diverse learning sources including traditional reference books, CD-ROMs, Web-Based Instruction, periodical indexes on and offline and analog video and analog sources.
- To provide learning experiences which teach students to become discriminating information consumers.
- To augment collaboration and assistance to classroom teachers in the field of informational literacy.
- To provide and familiarize students with information gathering learning experiences and activities which contribute to lifetime learning.
- To function as the information center and hub of the academic institution.
- To provide information gather activities and resources which provide a diversity of opinion, and a variety of social and cultural perspectives.

Webquest components

A WebQuest is an inquiry launched within internet sources of information. Structuring a Webquest for students involves six critical components:
- An introduction providing background information and objectives.
- A task which must be interesting and possible to achieve using online sources. The media specialist should know beforehand the areas of search and the information which will be retrieved.
- A clearly defined sequence of steps should begin a WebQuest.
- Students must be given instruction beforehand in how to organize and evaluate the information obtained. The credibility of various sources must be discussed.

Copyright © Mometrix Media. You have been licensed one copy of this document for personal use only. Any other reproduction or redistribution is strictly prohibited. All rights reserved.

- A WebQuest should have a conclusion. The conclusion should bring closure to the exercise, and reinforce what has been learned about the research topic.
- Task, process, evaluation and conclusions should be explained as separate processes.

Deep Web implications

'Invisible' or 'Deep Web' sources on the internet are depositories of information which are not routinely accessed by search engines. These sources are generally more complex and detailed than the general interest articles reached by common search engines like Yahoo and Google. Very often students are not aware of 'Invisible Web' sources (sometimes referred to as 'dark matter') nor are they aware of the means of accessing the information contained therein. The library media specialist should be well-versed in the various types of 'Deep Web' sources on the internet, and have a familiarity with the means of access and methods of organization of such material. Conventional search protocols do not reach 'deep matter' content for reasons of design or choice.

'Information literacy' components

An information literate person should have competency in the following skill sets:
- Research Process: Understanding the objectives, finding background information; identifying key concepts and related terms.
- Research Tools: An understanding of basic research tools involves the use of conventional search engines to find records and information. Search methods and techniques include Boolean searching, searches by phrase, subject, title, author, the use of 'wildcards' or truncated phrases.
- Finding Materials: Library catalogs, magazine indexes, search engines, public and private databases.
- Evaluation of Materials and Resources: Evaluations are based on credibility and timeliness of sources. Are the sources up-to-date? Are the sources reliable? Is there a 'Wiki' element to the information source?
- Responsible Usage of Resources: Avoid plagiarism by observing copyright and crediting rules both with regard to text and graphic information.

Website structure

Web interactive sites have a number of common structures which may be activated by the use of the mouse or arrow keys:
- Drop-down menus are some of the most basic structures and were earliest in development. Clicking on a drop-down menu provides additional navigation choices for the user.
- Screen arrows are a common method of computer interactivity which allow the user to move forward or backward as the learning or research progresses or needs reinforcement. Screen arrows are commonly used in tutorials.
- Menu trees are structures which resemble collapsible outlines of subject matter. Subject matter is usually organized into virtual folders represented by graphic icons. The user 'clicks' on the main headings of the menu tree to either expand or condense the topic into its main theme or headline.

School web page structures

Copyright © Mometrix Media. You have been licensed one copy of this document for personal use only. Any other reproduction or redistribution is strictly prohibited. All rights reserved.

Layout tables and Cascading Style Sheets (CSS) are two of the most important tools a library media specialist might use in constructing a library page or series of pages.

- <u>Layout tables</u> provide a template or form in which the site designer can lay out information topics and details in an organized way. Information provided in layout tables is concise and more easily read. Most often, the borders seen in layout tables are removed or made invisible after the web page is complete.
- <u>Cascading Style Sheets (CSS)</u> are a form of page formatting which relieves the tedium of specific line by line html programming. There are two chief advantages to the use of CSS formatting. The library media specialist can make changes in a single document and the information will 'flow' throughout other areas of the site. Another advantage is that more than one style sheet can be used within the document. Different levels of importance may then be assigned to major categories and sub-categories.

Social responsibility

A positive contribution to the learning community is an essential approach to information literacy. Three of the nine standards identified by the ALA as being necessary to information literacy for student learners fall under the category of 'social responsibility'.

- Social responsibility, in this context, means that the information literate student will be able to participate in groups to obtain and assemble information.
- The information literate person also recognizes how and why the spread of information is a vital component of democratic systems.
- Practicing ethical behavior in the treatment of information is a third concern which falls into the category of 'social responsibility' under ALA guidelines. Ethical behavior means observation of copyright rules and laws.

Program administration

Program administration refers to the activities which are vital and necessary to the collection, organization, evaluation, planning and management of a library media center. The collection of materials requires knowledge of print materials like books and periodicals, computer-based information materials like CD or online databases, and analog equipment. Printed materials must be properly organized according to the Dewey decimal system. Online sources must be linked and organized within the context of an 'interface'. In addition, collected information sources must be evaluated in terms of a school's educational objectives. Inappropriate materials must be weeded from the collection. Staff management is also a major part of any library administration program.

Planning activities

Six important planning activities for the library media specialist are:

- The library media specialist should convene a library advisory committee to obtain input from others who may be helpful in outline goals.
- The advisory committee and the library media specialist should work together to determine the library mission and philosophy.
- Goals and objectives should be set in clear terms.
- Plans formulated to achieve goals and objectives should be broken down into short and long-term goals.
- Programs should be evaluated in terms of their capacity to meet goals. The library media specialist must determine how and when the programs are to be delivered.

Copyright © Mometrix Media. You have been licensed one copy of this document for personal use only. Any other reproduction or redistribution is strictly prohibited. All rights reserved.

- Opportunities for collaboration with teachers, school administrators, and outside contacts should be addressed.

Needs assessment components

In assessing the needs of an educational institution and the means for reaching its goals, the library media specialist must:
- The needs of the school curriculum and student interests.   Library collections should focus in both areas.
- Implement and use collection mapping to augment availability of library resources.
- Surveys of staff and students are important in obtaining collaboration and cooperation from all parties working toward educational goals.
- Action research is required of the media specialist to determine costs, availability of space, and other elements which must be incorporated into library design plans.
- The media specialist will serve on curriculum committees in order to remain informed of curriculum initiatives and changes.
- Prioritization of needs is important and requires judgment. The media specialist should prioritize short-term goals while working toward long-term objectives.

Evaluating budgeting program

Budgetary issues are a fundamental concern in evaluating a school library administration program. Media specialists must obtain information about collection usage and service in order to properly evaluate the materials in the library collection.   Knowing what materials are being used and which are being ignored may lead to budget realization for the media specialist. Training of staff and students is critical and some part of the budget should be allocated for it. By the same token, additional materials purchases may be required to modernize and update the collection.   These types of concerns should figure into the evaluation of budget concerns and planning.

An appropriate budget should not be confused with a funded budget. The needs of students and curriculum providers should not be shortchanged because 'there are insufficient funds' in the overall budget.

Developing budget proposal

A budget proposal should be the product not only of the library media specialist, but of an entire committee comprised of teachers, administration representatives, and staff. A rationale for a specific budget proposal might be constructed considering the following elements:
- The information skills necessary to develop tomorrow's citizens in the workplace and in the society are paramount.
- The number of students and teachers who are to be served must be assessed and used in the development of a budget rationale.
- The library media specialist must consider outside funding sources for non-essential services the library may wish to provide.   Identify those separately in the budget submission, and explain their importance and viability.
- The library media specialist must be able to provide research to support budgetary decisions. Does the research support the likelihood of success in attainment of educational goals?

Copyright © Mometrix Media. You have been licensed one copy of this document for personal use only.
Any other reproduction or redistribution is strictly prohibited. All rights reserved.

- Subjective or sentimental decisions must be avoided in the budget process particularly when use patterns and educational research do not support the purchase of specific materials.

Staff management

The library media specialist must engage in a variety of staff management activities:
- Direct supervision of library staff including paid library aides. This involves scheduling and work assignments.
- Recruitment of student aides and volunteers are also part of staff management.
- Staff training must be an ongoing concern of the LMS. Past practices in staff training must be reevaluated and updated to reflect changes in technology and infrastructure. It is often necessary to design and implement new training strategies to reinforce and expand staff capabilities.
- Efficiency of operation must be a concern of the LMS. Operational procedures must be reviewed and revised when necessary. Services should be harmonious with teacher schedules and educational projects.

Process of 'reconsideration'

Reconsideration policy means that the LMS must establish procedures for addressing disputes with library users. Library staff must be fully knowledgeable and trained in reconsideration policy. The reconsideration process is the procedure whereby the user can bring complaint issues to higher levels of authority. The reconsideration process protects the library and its users from oversights and errors. The reconsideration process may have several steps, beginning with the initial determination. It is important that reconsideration of any issue be addressed in writing. To insure the integrity of the process, it is recommended that later steps in the process of reconsideration be addressed by persons other than those making the initial determination.

Circulation and selection policies

Circulation policy is the key to ensuring smooth operation of the library media center. Policies must be set regarding the time materials can be borrowed. The library media specialist must determine which materials (rare or historic, for example) may not be removed from library. Procedures for materials put on 'hold' must be established. Different procedures may be established for software and film.
Selection policy is vital and key to making the right choices in meeting the educational objectives of the school. Selection policy can be revised as school target objectives change. Inventory can be tracked for usage as a guide in determining the materials most frequently used. Selection policy should be the result of input from teachers, students, and from guidance provided by the school board.

Library media center concerns

Six concerns of the library media specialist who must plan a new library media center are:
- The facility should be designed with the view to creating a comfortable, safe, and inviting learning environment.
- Physical components and materials in the library should be selected and located in a way that will contribute to achieving educational goals.

Copyright © Mometrix Media. You have been licensed one copy of this document for personal use only. Any other reproduction or redistribution is strictly prohibited. All rights reserved.

- Select new technologies (software, hardware, and traditional media) which will engage a multiplicity of learning styles.
- Determine whether the existing facility is appropriate to meeting long-term and short-term goals.
- The LMS must be able to communicate library needs to architects, builders, school board members, and school administration. The facility should be designed around its function and target goals.
- Be sure that any planned new facility or renovation of an existing facility meets the criteria of the ADA (Americans with Disabilities Act)

Selection policy

The ALA Bill of Rights states that selection of material for the library should be universal and that no single point of view should be favored over another. Material selection must not reflect the choice or personal taste of a single individual but should express a divergence of views. In the mission of providing education and enlightenment, library media specialists have the responsibility of challenging censorship. In the attainment of that objective, libraries should resist all attempts to abridge free expression and free access to ideas. The ALA Bill of Rights advises libraries to equitably provide exhibit space for discussion, discourse, or the transference of information for all groups regardless of belief or affiliation.

Technology and confidentiality

Library media specialists are advised by the ALA to limit the degree to which personally identifiable information about an individual is collected, monitored, or distributed. This refers to web sites visited, registration (library cards) for use of facilities, and circulation records. The acronym PII (personal information identification) is used to describe the information gathering which is currently possible through the wide use of technology. Through credit card use, data entry of medical, intellectual, contact, or personal information, it is possible to construct a crude profile of an individual which may be used for purposes not intended by the individual user. The confidentiality aspect of the Library Bill of Rights is directed toward protecting the right to confidentiality of users and the right to free expression under the 1st Amendment.

Flexible scheduling

The AASL (American Association of School Librarians) recommends flexible scheduling of curriculum in order to effectively integrate school library programs with the school curriculum and objectives. A flexible school schedule allows teachers to coordinate with the library media specialist within the context of specific subject areas. Science or Language Arts projects can be taught more effectively in concert with the activity of developing library literacy skills. This is facilitated by flexible scheduling. Studies show that learning occurs at a more rapid pace when information literacy and subject curriculum are taught simultaneously. Administrators should build flexible scheduling into school management to support efforts at cooperative learning.

State confidentiality laws

Copyright © Mometrix Media. You have been licensed one copy of this document for personal use only. Any other reproduction or redistribution is strictly prohibited. All rights reserved.

State rules regarding confidentiality are in a state of flux and may be changed to reflect changes in technology. The American Library Association Library Bill of Rights provides advisory guidelines to protect client privacy and confidentiality of collected information. However, it is the responsibility of the library media specialist to consult with the school district's retained legal counsel when new confidentiality rules are mandated or previous rules are revised. Liabilities for improper implementation of privacy and confidentiality rules may be great and far-reaching, affecting teachers, schools, school boards and the entire school district. The school district's attorney is the best source for interpretation of new laws or revisions to rules and laws already in place.

Types of policies

Five types of media center policy which must be addressed and implemented by the library media specialist are:
- Acceptable-use policies define the uses to which library materials and information technology may be put. Acceptable use policy refers to the policy which guides students in the proper and ethical use of internet websites.
- Circulation policy provides the rationale for rules aimed at monitoring the borrowing of books and electronic materials.
- Confidentiality policy refers to the necessity of all staff to protect the privacy of library users. It may establish procedures for the handling of information and specify the strictly limited situations in which the information may be shared.
- Reconsideration policy refers to the procedures the library establishes for addressing complaints and disputes by users. Matters at issue may be reviewed by an independent panel or by staff having no previous contact with the issue.
- Selection policy refers to the choice of materials assembled and stored by the library. Selection policy determines the items which are to be 'weeded out' and other items which might be purchased to meet new goals.

Planning objectives

When planning and managing circulation activities, the library media specialist must consider:
- Accuracy: Records must be accurately kept in order to maintain efficient operation. Mistakes are costly in terms of time and personnel. Knowing who has possession of materials and where the materials are located and accessed is a vital function of the LMS.
- Access to materials: All legitimate users must have access to materials maintained in the school library. Rules must be established for access to specialized or rare materials. Access to personal records must be strictly evaluated with respect to the individual's right to privacy. Limitations must not be placed on usage due to age, origin, background, or viewpoints.
- Ease of patron use: Facilities must be freely available and the environment must be user friendly. Assistance should be provided to those having difficulty with access to materials. Care should be taken to provide access to persons with disabilities.
- Frequency of material usage is a key factor in evaluating library materials. Frequency of use may be affected by other factors like accessibility.

Assessing collection size

Copyright © Mometrix Media. You have been licensed one copy of this document for personal use only. Any other reproduction or redistribution is strictly prohibited. All rights reserved.

There are many factors which influence and determine the size of a school's library collection:
- Student and faculty needs should be addressed first. The size of the physical space, the student population, and the needs of teachers and administrators are of first concern.
- The LMS may inventory the number of titles held in each subject area to learn whether titles in one particular area may overbalance those in another area.
- Many educators will compare the size of a collection to the collections of other schools of similar size. Most states maintain statistics on the size of library collections and there are many private organizations which publish comparison studies.

Media program goals

Four important objectives of a school library media program are:
- The acquisition and distribution of materials.
- The ability to produce materials is important when library services must be directed toward a particular goal. Production of video tutorials may be one example where production of materials is desirable for individual and for staff general training.
- In-service training for staff is an ongoing responsibility of the library media specialist. The responsibility extends to permanent and part-time employees as well as to student aides and volunteer staff.
- Equipment acquisition must be pursued. Inventory of existing equipment should be scheduled periodically and regularly. It is important to ascertain whether equipment is working properly while conducting inventories of library equipment and stock materials.

Software technology

Four areas in which software technology can improve efficiency in a school library media center include:
- Task scheduling software. This software can be of great assistance in efficiently managing library staff work schedules. It can be easily stored and modified to accommodate changes in personnel and hours of operation. It efficiently stores records needed for payroll and other human resource purposes.
- Database software is useful is managing circulation records. It can combine and sort information by categories of date, type of materials, subject matter, and a variety of other categories which are useful in managing records and materials.
- Software product technologies are useful in inventory record-keeping. Data can be manipulated in a variety of useful ways and in accordance with selected categories.
- Production of overdue notices and other printing tasks is much more efficient through the use of technology. Notifications can be modified, printed, mailed and addressed without time-consuming hours devoted to manual tasks. Overdue notices or other communication between the library and its patrons can be sent via email as well.

Problems with OPAC

The acronym means Online Public Access Catalog (OPAC). It refers to the type of database adopted by most libraries in past years to convert physical card catalogue and periodical card data to online databases which can be searched by keywords and/or subject/and or title, etc. While OPACs are widespread, there are frequent complaints regarding search criteria. Some critics of the systems have called them 'myopic' because they too often rely on a narrow definition of search words or Boolean operators. There have been numerous modifications of the basic and early OPAC designs.

Copyright © Mometrix Media. You have been licensed one copy of this document for personal use only. Any other reproduction or redistribution is strictly prohibited. All rights reserved.

Modern OPACs allow 'wild-card' searching (using asterisks to represent missing search information, for example) and other features. A major change in OPAC design now concerns the degree of 'relevance' to data input for the initial search. The degree of relevance is often given as a percentage. The search results containing the highest percent of relevance may be the best place to look for specific information.

Design and location

Three important design criteria for locating a media center are:
- Central location: A media center would ideally be placed in an area where it is central to as many classrooms as possible. The ideal location would away from sources of noise distraction like cafeteria or music rooms.
- Consultation with users: Though there are several useful reference points for locating a school library collection, an important concern is to consult with the prospective users of the facility.
- Allowing space for future expansion: It is important to realize that budgeting is an ongoing incremental procedure. The LMS should focus on meeting current curriculum goals while allotting space for future expansion supported by new funding sources.

Online resources

Three common online information resources are:
- InfoTrac: An online database of journal articles maintained by Thomson Learning Corporation, a publisher of tests, textbooks, and educational media. The InfoTrac database incorporates thousands of full text articles from sources like the New York Times, scholarly journals and popular magazines.
- Encyclopedic Sources like Grolier's, World Book, Encarta, and Britannica are subscriber services often purchased by school libraries.
- CD Rom Sources: CD-ROMs are a varied collection of resources sold to educators and libraries for research purposes. Increasingly, the material covered by CD-Rom technology is being retrieved online. However, CD-ROMs can be focused and dedicated to a particular subject area, and may contain graphics, text, tutorials or other strategies directed toward specific goals in the school curriculum.

Hiring concerns

Training, background experience, and selection of a suitable candidate are the main concerns in hiring new staff in a media library center. The school human resources person must hire from a list of the best candidates. Very often a school will consider providing an intensive training program for persons within the school rather than head-hunting candidates from other schools. Whoever is hired will require training toward the specific facility goals of the new school environment.

Minimal staff of most school libraries is made up of a full-time library media specialist, adult volunteers, and student assistants. Since the staff of a library media center may consist of persons with different background and levels of education, a manual of procedures should be written, read, and used in new staff training.

URL extensions

Copyright © Mometrix Media. You have been licensed one copy of this document for personal use only. Any other reproduction or redistribution is strictly prohibited. All rights reserved.

URLs usually consist of a set of characters, a '.' or period, and a file extension. These file extension conventions are often recognizable. Identifying information is important to information research and saves time.

- **.gov**: This references a government information source. An example would be the Social Security website at ssa.gov
- **.edu**: This URL file extension is the one you'll see when searching schools and colleges for information. An example would be harvard.edu
- **.mil**: This type of site is a military site which may refer to websites like the pentagon, the Department of the Army, or other military sources. An example would be usarmy.mil
- **.com**: These are probably the most common URL file extensions and proliferate continuously with new 'dotcoms' coming online every day. They are private commercial sites operated for business purposes. An example would be ibm.com

Film clip extensions

Another type of graphic extension are the film clip types which may include .mpg; .mov; wmv and others. The type of file determines the software to be used for opening and viewing the file. Some software operates across 'platforms' and reads several or even all types of film clips. Other software platforms are capable of 'converting' one file type to another, but usually these are more expensive than some others. However, many hardware and software producers provide 'downloadable' limited versions of their products for free to encourage use and later purchase. Other products are 'freeware' and often supplied with the purchase of a computer. Having software that allows the researcher, teacher, or student to present short film presentations of educational subjects is an important part of any library center or education program.

New acquisitions strategies

Four strategies for promoting new acquisitions to the library media center are:

- The MLS may promote 'book talk' discussions to feature the newly acquired library materials.
- The MLS and student editors may wish to publish an article in the school newsletter or newspaper detailing how the new materials might be used.
- A gathering of teachers might be encouraged by invitation to a 'tea party' so that they can peruse new materials and discuss how the new materials may be used in a collaborative context.
- New materials can be presented graphically upon the bulletin board. Bulletin boards should be prominently located. Newly acquired books can be placed on holders and placed in visible locations so that their presence engages library visitors.

Bloom's Taxonomy

Benjamin Bloom was an educational psychologist at the University of Chicago. His work is useful to an understanding of student learning styles. Bloom outlined three 'domains' or areas of learning: affective, psychomotor, and cognitive. Bloom's Taxonomy identifies and outlines different levels of comprehension in student learning:

- Memorization is the first level of learning.
- Understanding may follow memorization but is not the highest level of comprehension, according to Bloom's learning model.

Copyright © Mometrix Media. You have been licensed one copy of this document for personal use only. Any other reproduction or redistribution is strictly prohibited. All rights reserved.

- Applying memorization and understanding to solve problems is the third level of learning, according to Bloom's Taxonomy.
- The final and highest levels of learning, according to Bloom's Taxonomy, is when the student acquires the skills of creativity, analysis, and evaluation.

Collection development

Five components of successful library collection development are:
- A library collection must represent multiple viewpoints on key issues. The reliability and currency of online sources is of continuing concern in assembling technology components of a collection.
- A library collection must reflect the various curriculums of the school program. All subject areas should be represented, including local historical sources of information.
- A library collection must remain current even as conditions change and the school provides strategies to deal with new requirements.
- A library collection must reflect the ethnic diversity of the student population.
- A library collection should accommodate special needs and those interesting in learning strategies for persons with emotional, learning, or physical handicaps.

Catalog sources

Four catalog sources which are useful in selecting books to acquire for the library collection media center are:
- School Library Journal - Founded in the 1950s, the School Library Journal is a monthly publication aimed at primary and secondary schools. It contains reviews of young adult titles and magazine articles pertaining to school library operations.
- Booklist - This catalog is available online or in print at the American Library Association website. It's published twice a month and much of it is geared to school and public libraries.
- The Horn Book – Another magazine featuring young adult fare for libraries. It's published in Boston and acts in the capacity of a gateway between publishers and purveyors of children's books for school libraries.
- Publisher's Weekly provides a review of pipeline fiction and non-fiction for children. Publishers of children's books and other materials submit their products to Publisher's Weekly months before a title is released for sale.

'MARC' record

MARC refers to machine readable cataloging and is a protocol whereby computers are able to read, sort, and output information regarding a library catalog. MARC is the foundation of most library catalogs in use in libraries of the United States. MARC is frequently criticized because its format is considered outdated, overly complicated, and cumbersome, yet there is currently no cataloguing protocol which has replaced it. There are several categories of MARC records. The ones most often seen in school and public libraries provide physical information about published sources: number of pages, publisher, date of publication, author, and other information. A MARC record may include a truncated topic description.

Evaluating non-fiction titles

Copyright © Mometrix Media. You have been licensed one copy of this document for personal use only. Any other reproduction or redistribution is strictly prohibited. All rights reserved.

Two important criteria used by the LMS in evaluating non-fiction titles for the library collection.

- Objectivity of the author - The author of a work intended for children should present the material in a way that does not over emphasize a single point of view. This is of particular concern in books with sociological content. A balanced point of view, or the display of an assortment of points of view, allows the learner to form a broader understanding of subject matter.
- Accuracy of the information - Accuracy is always a concern in non-fiction, particularly in the scientific fields. Part of information accuracy is the currency of the information provided. The fields of science, medicine, biology are frequently changing as additional research is conducted.

Organization protocols

Four different ways to organize a library collection are:

- MARC records are records which contain information about Title, Subject, Editor, Illustrator, and Translator. They are organized with the view to computer search techniques.
- Descriptive Cataloguing refers to a manner of organization often used in online materials organization. Chief sources of information in 'descriptive cataloguing' include the display of title pages, introductory screens, initial frames of filmstrips, and short film clips of longer films.
- General Fiction cataloguing is usually accomplished by alphabetical listing by the last name of the author.
- Dewey Decimal systems of classification provide a way of arranging collections by disciplines. Identifiable categories may be Art, Science, Medicine, or History, for example.

Genre literature

Genre literature means that the subject matter is of a particular type and often of a particular era. "American Gothic' is a genre, as is the 'Romance' novel. The LMS should be familiar with genre literature of various types. Other types of genre literature include:

- Fables: This is a type of genre literature in which animals or inanimate objects are cast in the same behaviors as humans, e.g., they can speak and interact in human terms. Fables usually have a moral tale to tell. Think of Aesop's fables.
- Fantasy: Fantasy literature has something in common with fables in that the unreal can happen. Objects and people can fly, just as wolves and foxes can speak. The difference is that there is rarely a moral and the kinds of fantastic things which can happen are limitless.

ICONnect

ICONnect is an online organization which has developed information exchange technologies in a variety of areas like health and education. In the field of education, ICONnect has four chief target goals:

- To promote library media programs as a way of disseminating information which will improve education and the public well-being.

Copyright © Mometrix Media. You have been licensed one copy of this document for personal use only. Any other reproduction or redistribution is strictly prohibited. All rights reserved.

- To provide families with educational resources and information vital to livelihood.
- To advance the principles of Information Power as a way of adapting to existing social and educational conditions.
- To offer free electronic courses with a view to furthering professional development of educators and librarians.

Children's award books

There are several awards given for literary works and to authors making a significant contribution to children's literature. Among them are:
- Hans Christian Anderson Award: This award is presented every two years. The award is given to recognize an author/illustrator's entire body of work.
- Newbery Award: Newbery Award winners include Lois Lowry's well known book THE GIVER, a tale of a futuristic society in which a teenage boy is given the position as 'keeper of the memories' in a society mired in orthodoxy and convention. Another Newbery award winner is Louis Sachar, who is known for the widely distributed book called HOLES. Sachar is the author of numerous books in the area of YA (young adult) fiction.
- Caldecott Awards: This award has been given twice to Chris Van Allsburg author/writer of the classic POLAR EXPRESS. David Wisniewski received the Caldecott for his unique illustrative style in his book GOLEM.

Online search concepts

Three online search concepts helpful to online researchers are:
- URL or internet web site extensions. These are a valuable clue to the type of site a person is searching. The URL extension .org indicates a non-profit organization, for example. Other extensions may indicate military, governmental, or commercial enterprise.
- Boolean logic. This is the type of logic used in forming on-line search strategies. Words and concepts bear a relationship to each other. These relationships are programmed into the computer Boolean search logic in order to obtain relevant results.
- Logical Operators like 'OR' and "AND" are used in online searches to narrow down the range of subjects retrieved. The use of these 'operators' cause the search engine to eliminate some of the irrelevant choices which may overwhelm the searcher.

OR, AND, NOT, and parentheses

These terms, known as logical operators, can be used to screen and manipulate information retrieved by an online search engine. Online search engines employ a type of logic called 'Boolean Logic'. Boolean logic references certain keywords related to the subject being researched. The degree of relationship between what is sought and what information is actually returned causes a great deal of difficulty, however. Putting in a single word or phrase or even two words strung together by 'AND' and/or 'OR' will generally result in a wide variety of retrieved items. Very often Boolean searches return too much information, much of it irrelevant.

Advanced Boolean searching might employ operators like 'NOT' and the use of parentheses. The researcher can specify which 'operators' are to be searched first. One of the ways to do this is to

Copyright © Mometrix Media. You have been licensed one copy of this document for personal use only. Any other reproduction or redistribution is strictly prohibited. All rights reserved.

place parts of the request in parentheses. The innermost parenthetical is searched first, and then the search expands outwards.

Equipment for visually impaired

Assistive equipment which may be used in the library to assist the visually impaired includes the following:

- Braille materials may be used as directional guidance around entrances and elevators. There are books and other instruction written with Braille characters. Braille is a form of raised writing which can be 'read' by sense of touch.
- Computer software coupled with voice synthesizers is becoming more common for use by the visually impaired. This may be an expensive but worthwhile solution to providing access to all students and faculty. Voice synthesis is also gaining popularity among those who are not visually impaired, so it is possible to justify the expense as 'dual purpose'.
- Specially marked signage can be strategically placed so as to mark entrances, elevators, bathrooms, and the location of computers and printed material.
- Kurzweil Reading Edge and the Kurzweil 1000 Reading systems are two products which aid the visually impaired in using library systems.

Technology assistance

An LMS might provide technology assistance to students in the school library in the following areas:

- A student may require assistance in downloading music or video files from online or CD-based instructional materials. The LMS must always monitor activity and inform students of the ethical use of information and the observance of copyright issues.
- A student may require assistance in obtaining permission from a company or publisher to use a music or text selection for research purposes.
- A student may need assistance in uploading a picture he/she has taken with a digital camera.
- A student may require assistance in sequencing and organizing a Power Point presentation. Visual presentations using presentation software like Power Point may involve insertion of outside digital photography and video.

Copyright © Mometrix Media. You have been licensed one copy of this document for personal use only. Any other reproduction or redistribution is strictly prohibited. All rights reserved.

Learning styles

Different learning styles have been part of educational psychology and teaching for decades. Learning style theories postulate that individuals learn in different ways.
- Visual learners profit most from learning exercises they can see, whether on the board, in print, or on the computer screen.
- Auditory learners profit most from oral instruction, or from audiotape. The theory holds that these students learn more rapidly when they 'hear' the lesson.
- Kinesthetic learners comprehend best by 'doing' the task that is to be learned.

The three basic learning styles have many variants, but the key concept to remember is that students have fundamental preferred styles of learning which will lead more quickly to goal achievement.

Distance education

Distance education is a method of teaching wherein the student is usually not in proximity to the teacher. Distance learning is a common feature of home schooling.
- Distance learning relies on technology for lesson delivery. Even with distance learning, there are times when the students and teachers come together in the same physical location.
- Programs and curriculum are controlled by an accredited educational institution. State requirements must always be met for advancement to upper grades.
- The process of disseminating information is dependent upon electronic or other media. In the past, distance learning was delivered through regular mail. Now, educational materials may be presented on a website, through television, by podcast and other technologies.
- A method of two-way communication is always required between teacher and student. Email, video, audio tapes, telephone, and occasional meetings can all be a part of distance learning.

Poetry Month

Children may be more easily drawn to poetry when the instructor is aware of the following literary elements:
- Selected poems should have exciting meters and rhythms which will hold the attention of young learners. Poems like the 'Midnight Ride of Paul Revere' stick in memory because the rhythms emulate the action of the poem.
- The use of sharp visual images can stimulate young minds to focus on poetic works.
- Odd language and humor contribute to literature appreciation by young students. Words used in fresh, new ways are attractive to children who are acquiring vocabulary skills along with poetry appreciation.
- The teacher's and librarian's choice of poems should allow for interpretation and vicarious living. Select poetry that allows children to enter the poetic context.

Information literacy plans

Information literacy must be part of a larger learning plan which encompasses a history, language arts, science or other curriculum lesson. Defining the lesson objective is the first step. It applies as much to the library media specialist as it does to the teacher administering the lesson. It is important that teacher and the library media specialist be absolutely clear about what is to be

Copyright © Mometrix Media. You have been licensed one copy of this document for personal use only. Any other reproduction or redistribution is strictly prohibited. All rights reserved.

accomplished and work together toward achieving the goal. The lesson objectives should incorporate the teacher's specific curriculum objectives within the context of information literacy. The use of technology or print materials cannot be taught in isolation.

Motivational steps

The motivational steps follow after the lesson objectives are defined. Motivation must stimulate student interest and response. Motivational objectives may be focused on illuminating background personal experience of the students. The use of visual stimuli followed by a question-response or group discussion might be a good way of jump starting a lesson regarding the use of imagery and language in video game technology, for example. It helps to motivate students when the teacher and library media specialist use techniques which rely on background information and learning already acquired. The motivational aspect of a teaching lesson must not focus on a presumed common background experience. The motivational aspect of a teaching plan should reflect diversity and openness to a variety of background experience.

Lesson summaries

Whether the subject area being taught is language arts, science, biology, history, geography, it is important to reinforce what is learned by means of a summary. The summary should meld all the elements which have been learned and the technologies which have been used. A geography lesson might have the targeted objective of teaching about the Grand Canyon, for example. The classroom teacher has reviewed weather, topography, and significant facts in the classroom. In the library media center, the students have been motivated by an online presentation of the visual scene using a technology like Google Earth. The class has been broken up into small groups, each of which has been encouraged to provide an oral report with a spokesperson selected by the group. All of the activities summarize the body of learning in the teacher's subject area and in the area of information literacy. The content of the entire lesson must be reviewed and reinforced.

Evaluation methods

Evaluation of library media plan objectives can be made in a variety of ways.
- Traditional methods include testing and quizzes, and these are not to be disregarded as they provide standard measures of the levels of learning success.
- Application of the tools acquired in the lesson can be tested by having students duplicate the results of a previous lesson with new material. In this way, the LMS can see if the students are able to apply knowledge gained in the previous lesson plan.

Example: Students used a combination of online and offline technology and classroom teaching to explore the Grand Canyon. The students are then given the broader topic of the 'American Southwest' and instructed to use the same resources to develop information, write reports, and present oral dissertations on the subject. This would be another way of evaluating the effectiveness of the collaboration efforts of teacher and LMS.

Encouraging reading

Current research shows that the most effective means of encouraging elementary school children is to have a wide variety of interesting reading material available in the environment. Reluctant

Copyright © Mometrix Media. You have been licensed one copy of this document for personal use only. Any other reproduction or redistribution is strictly prohibited. All rights reserved.

readers tend to favor newspapers, magazines and series books in which they already have an interest.

The use of animals as characters in a story is also a very effective means of getting younger children to develop interest in reading. Animals are the basis for Aesop's fables and many a children's story like Goldilocks and the Three Bears. Most children will have some connection and fascination with animals so it may be easy to encourage reading through the study of animals or stories with animals as one of the characters.

Collaboration

A collaboration between a library media specialist and a fifth grade teacher must begin with a solid lesson plan and proceed through various levels of understanding and knowledge building.
- The classroom teacher might motivate the students by establishing groups and have the students describe the characteristics and behavior of various species that they know of.
- The library media specialist might take groups of ten to the media center for instruction on information retrieval. The LMS might shows students how to get information on what animals eat, where animals live, and what animals are endangered.
- The classroom teacher might provide blank outline maps and instruct students to fill in the areas where species of animals may be found.
- The library medial specialist's collaboration might consist of using computer graphic arts or publishing programs to design brochures showing how animal species must be protected.

Students with special needs

Special needs students may be accommodated in the following ways:
- The granting of extra time to accomplish tasks. Additional break time might also benefit special needs students, as oftentimes these students are easily frustrated.
- The visually or auditory impaired may benefit from being seated closer to the subjects being taught and closer to the person teaching the subject. Special needs students work well in an environment which accommodates their limitations.
- A teacher or library media specialist should consider the use of assistive devices where warranted.
- A student with a motor impairment might be accommodated by allowing the student to take tests verbally rather than in writing.

Many different strategies exist for accommodating special needs students, but it must be stressed that such students cannot be allowed to avoid test-taking.

Using website information

With the wide availability of data within online sources and the proliferation of 'cut and paste' software and editing tools, it is important that students obey rules and ethics of copyright.
- When web-site materials authored by others are used in reports or other publication, students must check the copyright statement exhibited on the website.
- Whenever graphics or direct quotes are used in school reports, credit must be given to the website authors and the reference must be clearly stated in the bibliography.

Copyright © Mometrix Media. You have been licensed one copy of this document for personal use only. Any other reproduction or redistribution is strictly prohibited. All rights reserved.

- The student should obtain permission from the website to use the material. Contact with website developers or producers can easily be made by email or phone contact. The student may wish to consult with the library media specialist in this regard.

Big6 information

Big6 information is a methodology developed for the acquisition of information literacy skills. It a six-step process:
- Task Definition: This step consists of defining the educational problem and the information needed.
- Information Seeking Strategies: This consists of retrieving many sources of information and choosing the best ones to use.
- Location and Access: This refers to physical sources, whether the source is the school or outside libraries, books, online databases or websites.
- Using the Information: This step involves extracting the information about the topic being researched. The material must be sorted by priority, currency, and relevancy.
- Synthesis: Synthesis means taking the information obtained from the various sources and using it in a presentation, either written, oral, or both.
- Evaluation: Evaluation involves judging the effectiveness of the research. Does it accomplish the objectives of learning established in the lesson plan?

Assessment techniques

Information literacy can be measured in traditional and non-traditional ways.
- Applying a 'rubric' is a manner of assessing information literacy. Rubrics are useful in making assessments of such tasks as research and report writing.
- Conventional testing is a traditional way of evaluating student progress toward information literacy. This is often criticized in that it tends to measure memorized rather than applied skills.
- Journal entries are another method wherein a student's information literacy can be assessed. Journal entries have the advantage for the student of being composed in the quiet of a library or the privacy of a home.
- A one-on-one conference by the LMS with each individual student can reveal a student's mastery of information literacy. The student can directly report on areas of concern which need further development.

Public relations objectives

Public relations objectives of a school or community library program may be assisted by:
- Surveys of the community's attitudes and perceptions regarding the school library are important tools which provide a platform for a public relations outreach strategy.
- Newsletter publications are a great way of communicating this information to the public. Communities should be regularly informed regarding the types of activities which are conducted in the school library as well their impact on student learning.
- Parents and students can be solicited to volunteer in media center programs.
- Direct communication with members of the public community at school board meetings is a way of communicating media center needs as well as information about student achievement.

Copyright © Mometrix Media. You have been licensed one copy of this document for personal use only. Any other reproduction or redistribution is strictly prohibited. All rights reserved.

Community resource files

It is the responsibility of the school library media specialist to maintain a central location for records and information pertaining to community services, agencies, and facilities which function for the public good. Among the records in a community resource file, one might expect to find:

- A directory of public speakers who may be called upon to deliver information to community groups.
- The addresses and telephone numbers local businesses and government facilities host educational field trips or conduct facility tours for educational purposes.
- The addresses of public libraries and/or media collections in the local area should also be maintained.
- The location of museums and other cultural institutions should be maintained in the school library community resource files.

Skill standards

The ALA and the AASL have proposed eight skill standards to be met in preparation for the school library media specialist position. Among them are these five:

- The school library media specialist should be a knowledgeable teacher. Effective library collaboration requires knowledge of teaching practice and curriculum in addition to library skills.
- The school library media specialist should be capable and knowledgeable in constructing a plan for the building of a collection.
- The school library media specialist should be expert in information retrieval, dissemination, and organization.
- The school library media specialist must be a skilled manager. The school LMS must manage permanent and volunteer staff as well as public relations activities.
- Since the technology and academic environments are always changing and developing, the school library media specialist must be a lifelong learner.

Freedom to Read Statement

The ALA Freedom to Read statement advocates for the widest possible freedom to read in libraries. It has seven points which discourage censorship or filtering regardless of the age, culture, or background of the library patron. The ALA statement is used as a basis for promoting an annual Banned Books Week to promote freedom in reading. It supports public resistance to citizens groups attempting to require filters on library computers. It supports an Office on Intellectual Freedom. The ALA statement proposes that free reading is integral to democratic political functioning. It states that citizens in a democracy are themselves capable of distinguishing between fact and propaganda, between good and evil. The ALA Freedom to Read statement is an idealistic one, inspired by an appreciation for individual freedom.

CIPA

The Children's Internet Protection Act (CIPA) was introduced into the congress in 1999. Its purpose was to protect children from online pornography and contact with sexual predators. CIPA was immediately subject to a series of challenges by the American Library Association. The bill was signed into law by President William Clinton in December of 2000. Challenges to the filtering and censorship provisions of the law moved through the courts to the level of the U.S. Supreme

Copyright © Mometrix Media. You have been licensed one copy of this document for personal use only. Any other reproduction or redistribution is strictly prohibited. All rights reserved.

Court.   The CIPA was upheld by the Supreme Court in June of 2003 in spite of ALA's attempts to have it declared unconstitutional.   However, the Children's Internet Protection Act has provisions which allow local libraries to enforce reasonable standards of protection.   Federal and state government entities are barred from censorship activities in accordance with this law.   Earlier attempts at web-filtering software in public and school libraries were judged by the Supreme Court to abridge 1st Amendment rights.

Copyright © Mometrix Media. You have been licensed one copy of this document for personal use only.
Any other reproduction or redistribution is strictly prohibited. All rights reserved.

Professional Teaching Standards

The mission of the National Board for Professional Teaching Standards was established in 1987. Its purpose was to elevate national teaching standards to meet higher academic goals:

- It proposed high and rigorous standards for what certified teachers should be able to do and accomplish.
- It established a system whereby teachers and MLS could voluntarily obtain a national certification which would maintain uniformly high standards in all the states of the country.
- It advocates educational reforms which would utilize nationally certified teachers to advance educational programs in the classroom and in information media centers.

According to the ALA, approximately 40,000 teachers have obtained National Board Certification.

NBPTS core propositions

Five core propositions of the NBPTS standards include:

- The proposition that teachers are committed to students and learning is fundamental to the NBPTS standards. The standards reflect the proclivity and motivation of teachers to advance education as a means of social improvement.
- A second proposition is that teachers develop the best means of teaching their students, and that they are familiar with the subjects they teach.
- Teachers are effective and responsible managers of student learning.
- Teachers are organized and systematic in their teaching procedures, adapting their lessons to their practical experience in the classroom.
- Teachers function within the larger educational community to advance curriculum goals. They share resources and materials, exchange information, and participate in organizations which advance the goals of information literacy.

Computer technology skills

There are several basic technology functions which should be known to all library media specialists:

- Setting up a personal computer, connecting components like printers and installing software.
- Knowledge of basic operating system functions. Software and hardware maintenance including the use of disk utilities like defragmentation and disk compaction.
- Software familiarity: word processing applications; database software; spreadsheets; graphics and/or desktop publishing software.
- Setting up and using internet connections to communicate with others and to locate information and resources.
- Using instructional materials consisting of print and online documentation of new features and applications.
- Connecting a computer to a network. With the proliferation of wireless network hardware, the installation of networks becomes more facile and widespread. Library media specialists and Nationally Board Certified Professional teachers should be familiar with network administration software.

Standard 1 literacy skills

Copyright © Mometrix Media. You have been licensed one copy of this document for personal use only. Any other reproduction or redistribution is strictly prohibited. All rights reserved.

Students must reach standard 1 information literacy levels in Grades 3 to 5. The students understand that behavior is learned from others. Comprehension of behavior stems from experience, from conversation with others, from role modeling behavior, and from directed observation. Books, television, film, and online sources contribute to information literacy in the content area of Behavioral Studies within these grade levels.

Standard 1 information literacy standards for groups in Grades 9 through 12 in the Health content area means that the students know local, state, federal and private agencies entrusted with protecting and informing the consumer. Students within these grades meeting standard 1 will be able to accurately respond to questions in this content area.

Standard 2 criteria

The ability to evaluate information critically and competently meets Standard 2 requirements for information literacy. The indicators of this competency are accuracy, relevance, and comprehensiveness. Within the Standard 2 criteria, there are different levels of accomplishment. Students may meet basic Standard 2 levels or become proficient. The highest standard 2 criteria for information literacy would result when students are able to balance and measure conflicting data and research, resolving and constructing solid rationales for information gathering tasks. Students operating at the highest level of proficiency would be quick to differentiate fact from opinion and point of view. High levels of standard 2 information literacy are required to address controversial topics for which there is a variety of opinion based on similar data.

Collaboration, leadership and technology

The library media specialist is an integral part of the instructional partnership between school, classroom teacher, and the library media center. The LMS teaches, guides students in providing information access, and administers and manages the library programs. Student learning is at the core of all programs, and the library media center is the area where all efforts are joined. In this context, the LMS must establish a positive ongoing relationship with teachers and inspire teachers to use all available library resources. The LMS should enlist the teacher's help in making the connection between content and library technology, being persistent and flexible in time-budgeting and the scheduling of available staff.

Copyright © Mometrix Media. You have been licensed one copy of this document for personal use only. Any other reproduction or redistribution is strictly prohibited. All rights reserved.

Leadership skills

Leadership for the school library media specialist has the following characteristics:
- Leadership for the LMS has been described as the responsibility of 'leading from the middle'. Leading from the middle means being a link between the student seeking information, the classroom teacher, and the technology which will deliver information.
- Leadership direction by the LMS means using available technology for inventory, updating, information retrieval, and for accomplishment of curriculum goals.
- The library media specialist's leadership is directed toward building a successful educational team of teachers and administrators, and to partnering with the outside community.

Principles of learning and teaching

The ten principles of learning and teaching identified by the AASL for the school library media program.
- Principle One –the library media literacy program must be integrated with the school curriculum to promote student success and achievement.
- Principle Two – Information literacy is an integral part of the school's content and curriculum objectives.
- Principle Three - Modeling and promoting collaboration in planning and curriculum development.
- Principle Four - Modeling and promoting collaborative teaching in creative and effective ways.
- Principle Five - A fundamental of learning is full access to information and resources of the library media center.
- Principle Six - To encourage and involve students in reading, viewing and listening for enjoyment and comprehension.
- Principle Seven - To support the diverse learning styles, needs, and abilities of students and other members of the learning community.
- Principle Eight - To foster individual and learning community inquiry.
- Principle Nine - To integrate usage of technology for learning and teaching.
- Principle Ten - To serve as a vital link to the larger communities of learning.

Successful intellectual work

Successful intellectual work, as defined by the National Board for Professional Teaching Standards means:
- Construction of Knowledge: Requires higher-order thinking skills to develop new meanings from retrieved library resources. This is more desirable than merely reproducing and repackaging information obtained from print and online sources.
- Disciplined Inquiry: Refers to the kind of rigorous intellectual approach necessary for successful interpretation and comprehension of content areas. Disciplined inquiry means the exploration of links between information sources in order to solve problems rather than to memorize content.
- Connections Beyond School – This is an information skill necessary for success in intellectual work because it has value beyond good grades in schoolwork. Individuals

Copyright © Mometrix Media. You have been licensed one copy of this document for personal use only. Any other reproduction or redistribution is strictly prohibited. All rights reserved.

with 'connections beyond school' solve real-world problems and become influences upon and advocates for educational goals beyond school.

Reference sources

There are several highly esteemed reference sources which are of help in the operation of the library media center.

- The book 'Information Power' is a compilation published jointly by the AASL and AECT. AASL is the American Association of School Librarians. AECT is the acronym for Association for Educational Communications and Technology.
- Another well-known reference source is Loertscher's 'Taxonomies of the School Library Media Program'.
- A third useful book is published by Gillespie and Spirt: Administering the School Library Media Center.
- A voluminous series of books of reference for the library media center is the six-volume set titled 'School Library Media Annual'.

Research actions

Whether you are a Nationally Board Certified Library Specialist (NBCLS) or preparing for National Board Certification (NBCT), program administration in a library media center is a daunting task. Beginning research and evaluation of existing media center resources is a good first step.

- Study any previous written evaluation by media personnel or improvement committees, library committees, or even annual reports.
- Conduct an informal survey of teachers to gather input about their perceptions of past practices and needs for collection.
- Make a list of questions which arise from your review of the existing facility and review your list against the recommendations of the National Board for Professional Teaching Standards.
- Produce a written evaluation of all your research. Meet with a committee of teachers, library staff, interested school board members, and any library parent/teacher committee members to formulate an improvement plan.

Information specialist roles

The three roles defined by the AASL in conjunction with AECT are the information specialist, the teacher specialist, and the instructional consultant. All three roles are combined in the single person of the library media specialist.

- The information specialist communicates with learning communities to implement technology based and print-based learning strategies. The information specialist provides instruction and guidance in the functioning of information retrieving systems and assures that the physical facility can be accessed by all.
- The teacher specialist plans activities with the classroom teacher. The teacher specialist also conducts staff development and establishes procedures for media production and technology use.
- The instructional consultant assists teachers in acquiring information and technology skills needed in support of classroom instruction.

Challenges to intellectual freedom

Copyright © Mometrix Media. You have been licensed one copy of this document for personal use only. Any other reproduction or redistribution is strictly prohibited. All rights reserved.

Controversial issues in our society include gay rights, pornography, profanity, the battle over creationism vs. evolution, sex education, racism, violence in media and others. It is important not to panic if a member of the public should raise an issue with the school or public library. The following steps should be taken:

- Politely advise the complainant that their concerns will be considered and invite the person to file a formal complaint in writing. Any formal complaint should express specific concerns.
- Inform school administrators or the public library chief executive that a complaint has been filed. The school board attorney should be duly informed, and the matter sent to the reconsideration or reviewing board.
- The reconsideration or reviewing board will decide whether the matter can be reasonably settled. If not, the reviewing board will meet with the school attorney to recommend a policy and a prescribed course of action.

Copyright laws

The proliferation of copy equipment and cut and past word processing has put new strains on copyright laws. School and public libraries should be aware of basic principles, laws, and ethics regarding the use of published material.

- The school district may have published its own policy strictly delineating its copyright policies.
- Teachers and media specialists may have been provided with a 'manual' either online or in print to underscore the problems which arise in the copyright area.
- Educators are provided extra leeway in the interpretation of copyright law. The 'brevity' test allows teachers or the LMS to copy a complete essay, story, or excerpts of no more than 1000 words or 10% of a work (whichever is less). Copying that does not meet the 'brevity test' cannot be copied for use in the classroom unless authorization is obtained from the publisher and author.

Doctrine of 'fair use'

Teachers are allowed use of published copyrighted material for academic and classroom purposes so long as they meet the criterion of 'fair use'. 'Fair use' considers the needs of learners against the protections of copyright. However, the defining characteristic of 'fair use' is that copying published material cannot be done to advance commercial purposes. So long as there is no intent to deprive the author of a work of profit, then 'fair use' of the material is permitted.

Different and more complex rules may apply with the proliferation of computer software materials. It is best to heed the specific rules plainly stated on the packages of software providers.

The showing of video-taped productions is yet another area where challenges arise. 'Fair use' of a video production is a matter which should be addressed by written school policy or by the school attorney.

Copyright violations

There are specific steps to follow in the instance of a suspected copyright violation by a teacher or staff member.

Copyright © Mometrix Media. You have been licensed one copy of this document for personal use only. Any other reproduction or redistribution is strictly prohibited. All rights reserved.

- Determine first whether a violation has positively occurred. Seek advice or consultation until the issue is clear and before bringing the matter to higher authorities.
- Inform the violator to cease the activity. Explain why and how it is a violation of copyright. Present the information constructively and invite agreement rather than confrontation.
- If further infractions should occur after the media specialist's attempt to halt the violations, then the matter should be brought up to the educator's supervisor to determine the appropriate course of action.
- In situations where the potential copyright violation was reported by other library staff (and in most cases it would be), it is important to inform the reporter that the matter is being addressed. It is also proper to explain the results or outcomes of the reported activity.

Instructional duties

The library media specialist is always in the role of an instructor. While the amount of structured library teaching varies with the age group being taught (it will often be greatest with elementary school children who cannot work independently), the library media specialist is expected to actively instruct in the following areas:
- Train students in the retrieval of information. This type of training would involve traditional print materials, periodical catalogues, and online sources.
- Train students to recognize different media formats and the varied ways in which information is displayed and maintained in online catalogues.
- Train and instruct students in the methods of critical thinking. Students must be taught to prioritize information sources according to accuracy, currency, and relevant content.
- Demonstrate how information skills learned contribute to citizenship responsibilities.

Process design steps

The LMS must follow certain steps in planning, designing and then evaluating a library video or audio tutorial.
- The purpose or objective of a tutorial is the first thing that should be made clear. The LMS should define what is to be taught and what level of proficiency will be required of the targeted audience.
- The LMS must then determine the needs and abilities of the target audience. Identifying the target audience is the second step in tutorial design. Consider the age and level of learning of the target group. Consider learning styles and interests as well as learning needs.
- There must also be a means of evaluating the efficacy any media product. If the instructional video or audio product fails to show an effective outcome, it must be revised. The ability to perform a task without additional instruction is a measure of the effectiveness of the tutorial product.

Library budgeting team

The library media specialist should always volunteer to be part of the library budgeting team with a focus upon the following areas:
- The LMS should always keep abreast of new trends and studies regarding the curriculum goals in order to integrate new trends into future educational objectives. The library

Copyright © Mometrix Media. You have been licensed one copy of this document for personal use only. Any other reproduction or redistribution is strictly prohibited. All rights reserved.

media specialist should volunteer to serve on curriculum committees, including those entrusted with review of budget matters.

- School media professionals need to consider state department of education or other legislated standards with regard to budget needs.
- The LMS must also assist in prioritizing media center program goals. Within that context, the LMS must be able to assess the costs of meeting separate categories and present these projections to the committee for discussion and review.

Replacement cost formulas

There are various budget formulas which may be employed by school and public libraries as guidelines for budget committee recommendations. The general factors to consider are student population trends, and attrition of materials by loss, outdating, or other weeding. There are recommended formulas for replacement costs of a library print collection.

- Replacement costs formula multiplies the number of books in a collection by the average cost of books multiplied by 5%.
- (5% X Number of Books X Average Cost of Book)
- Periodical replacements cost estimates uses the same formula but substitutes 'Average Subscription Price' for 'Average Cost of Book'.

Standardized policies

Policies regarding circulation must be standardized and well-publicized. Rules should be displayed where users can review them in order to prevent disputes which require time and money to address.

- A policy must be set regarding the use or loan of historical or rare materials. There may be different loan periods for different materials.
- Staff should be trained in the fair and equal implementation of materials borrowing policy.
- Important reference materials may also have limitations placed upon the loan period. A policy regarding the number of these materials which can be borrowed must be set as well as the length of time for borrowing them.
- A process must be established for handling overdue, lost, or destroyed materials.
- Security provisions must be established and library staff must be trained in security systems. The use of theft detection devices must be implemented. Opening and closing times and procedures must be set.

Automated circulation systems

Speed and ease of handling are good reasons for automated circulation systems. The use of barcodes and scanning devices assists in maintaining records of inventory. There is a great savings in storage space traditionally occupied by cumbersome card files. With automated systems, it is easier and faster to evaluate the collection or manipulate record categories and types. Similarly, usage statistics can be monitored more accurately.

The advantages of an automated system cannot be challenged by traditional systems, yet there are some concerns which may be disadvantageous. Automated systems use electric power. Backup energy systems are required to prevent loss of data during power interruptions. Automated systems may be compromised by 'hacking' or by careless handling of confidential information.

Copyright © Mometrix Media. You have been licensed one copy of this document for personal use only. Any other reproduction or redistribution is strictly prohibited. All rights reserved.

Bibliographic record listing

The five components of a standard bibliographic record listing are:
- Call Number: the DDC (or LCNN) classification number and book number consisting of numbers and letters.
- Author Heading: A record can be searched by using the name of the author as it appears here.
- Title and Publishers/Illustrators - Includes Titles, and Sub-titles, as well as translators, illustrators, editors functioning in decision making with regard to text.
- Notes: The 'notes' section of a bibliographic record contains pertinent information about the type of material in which information is presented. It might identify an item as an audio or videotape or computer program, for example.
- Physical Description: This part of the record shows the number of pages, describes the use of illustrative matter. It may mention accompanying CD-ROMs with certain book editions, for example.

Big6 steps and plans

The Big6 process consists of six steps: task definition; information seeking strategy; location and access; use of information; synthesis; and evaluation.
- Task Definition: We're looking for information about the famous historical Walking Purchase for a research report.
- Information Seeking Strategies: We will use library online resources, museum and historical websites, and books.
- Location and Access: We've discovered a local Indian museum which has a collection of historical documents relating the Walking Purchase. We used the SIRS database, and several books we've found on Pennsylvania history.
- Use of Information: Keep records and document all sources, even the conversation you had with the museum director who assisted you in locating historical documents. Be especially careful to document online sources correctly and patiently.
- Synthesis: Organize the information. Prioritize the material on the basis of relevance. Make short written reports of the various categories and lay them out with a view to overall perspective.
- Evaluation: What could you have done better? Is there additional information resources you might have used? Could you have eliminated less relevant information?

Information seeking strategies rubric

A rubric is a series of benchmarks which measures student progress in achieving a task objective. It defines different levels of ability. In the area of Locating Information and Developing Information Strategies, a rubric might contain four levels or benchmarks:
- Basic Level – The teacher or LMS selects information resources. The student can little differentiate or evaluate materials used.
- Functional Level - The student selects resources but they are not always relevant. Priorities are confused. The student tends to follow a single track in the use of resources.
- Proficient Level - Student uses a wide variety of information resources. Good organization and focus of materials. Student pays attention to and records bibliographic data.

Copyright © Mometrix Media. You have been licensed one copy of this document for personal use only. Any other reproduction or redistribution is strictly prohibited. All rights reserved.

- Advanced Level - Student always selects relevant information. Research data is organized in terms of priority and relevance. Bibliographic references are complete. A clear timeline is apparent in the data collection activities. Materials are current and relevant to objectives.

Research product rubric

A rubric is a series of benchmarks which measures student progress in achieving a task objective. Information literacy requires students to be able to evaluate their production of information sources and collected data. Various levels of proficiency may be defined:
- Basic Level - The student is content with completing the assignment. Student has little idea how to improve quality. The student does not work beyond basic elements of task. The student requires outside input to evaluate and make suggestions.
- Functional Level - The student completes basic elements of task but sees where future projects could be improved. Student recognizes weaknesses in data collection and organization.
- Proficient Level - Student revises appropriately, organizing material in terms of relevance, currency, and accuracy. Student is yet unsure of the presentation of the material.
- Advanced Level – The student finds weaknesses in organization and collection and revises with a view to creating a better product. Revisions are appropriate, not merely a repetition of prior misconceptions. Information is abundant and factual. The student uses information creatively and has a thorough understanding of topic.

Group functioning rubric

Group functioning in Information Literacy can be categorized and measured in accordance with the following rubric:
- Basic Level - Students does not actively participate, exhibits passive compliance with other group members.   Sometimes distracts the group effort.
- Functional - Accommodates the group when urged by others, but shows little initiative. Offers information but it may be less relevant, less current, and less accurate than student operating at higher levels.
- Proficient - Student locates information needs and contributes them to group efforts. Assists in referencing and organization but does not show leadership. Information is accurate and timely.
- Advanced – Shows leadership in information gathering. Suggests data resources which can be used and discusses them with other group members. Leads the group and negotiates group conflicts and differences of opinion. Has acquired a thorough knowledge of topic area.

Ethical use of information

Ethical use of information content and sources requires that students give credit to others when using information. Students must know when to use quotation marks if they are unable to put information in their own words. Responsible use means that the student understands why content cannot be plagiarized or copied. Copying computer disks, tapes, or other digital materials is illegal without permission of the owner. A bibliography must also credit the source of the information used. The information literate student understands that ideas are not subject to copyright, yet is

Copyright © Mometrix Media. You have been licensed one copy of this document for personal use only. Any other reproduction or redistribution is strictly prohibited. All rights reserved.

able to make the distinction that copying style and content of material does constitute copyright violation.

First amendment

The First Amendment of the U.S. Constitution protects the right of free speech. The principle of 'intellectual freedom' means respect for what others read in print and listen to or watch in broadcast, or on computer outlets. The student who respects intellectual freedom of others will not act to prevent expression of ideas which they may not hold themselves. Part of intellectual freedom is to offer and express one's own opinion in an appropriate manner. The student with a deep understanding of First Amendments rights and the principles of intellectual freedom also knows and understands the legal avenues to follow in protecting those rights.

Learning community collaboration

In the modern world of information technology, research does not take place in a single location. It occurs in a larger world of interconnected resources beginning with the public or school library and extending outward. The LMS is expected to be aware of collaboration between learning communities. The LMS actively assists in the extension of collaboration by equipping, outfitting, and planning central activities toward far reaching information literacy goals. Information literacy extends outwards from student centered library activities to the larger community of learners. The larger community of learners consists of teaching staff and administration, parents, family, the local community, district and state offices and agencies, professional associations and national resources, international and global resources.

Collaborative links

The learning community is comprised of linked groups:
- At the core of the learning community are students learning about information literacy.
- The school's teaching staff, including the LMS and the library staff, forms the next link in the information chain of the learning community. The teaching staff is directly involved in communication and literacy instruction.
- The third link in the learning community consists of parents, community facilities like historical societies and local museums, public libraries, and local agencies which disseminate information on environmental, historical, cultural and other issues.
- The fourth link of the learning community consists of state educational facilities, state universities, and federal agencies which collect information and disseminate research information.
- A host of national professional associations maintain and disseminate information to members. These associations, groups, or organizations comprise the outer web of the learning community.
- The outermost learning circle in the web of collaboration among learning communities are the many International and Global organizations dedicated to education and information literacy.

ICONnect, KIDSConnect, and LM_NET

Copyright © Mometrix Media. You have been licensed one copy of this document for personal use only. Any other reproduction or redistribution is strictly prohibited. All rights reserved.

There are a number of technological resources designed to expand information literacy beyond the boundaries of the school and community libraries. ICONnect, KIDSConnect, and LM_NET are resources designed to provide young students with information connections.

- ICONnect is aimed at teachers and library staff. It is operated by AASL (American Association of School Libraries) and has the mission of broadening information skills and making better use of electronic information.
- KIDSConnect is a sub-category of ICONnect. It is geared toward the K-12 group. KIDSConnect provides a network of volunteers who provide technical assistance to students seeking information. KIDSConnect staff and volunteers may be contacted for assistance by email.
- LM_NET is sponsored by ERIC (Educational Resources Information Center). ERIC is a U.S. sponsored government database of bibliographic information. LM_NET allows media specialists and teachers to share information and ideas in a web-connected global environment.

Technology not an end

Principle 9 of the Learning and Teaching Principles for school library media programs defines technology as a 'product' and a 'process' used in learning and teaching, not as an objective in itself.

- 'Product' refers to the wide array of hardware and software available to facilitate learning and teaching. Software, hardware, audio, visual or interactive materials are tools used in the retrieval, organization, and evaluation of information sources.
- 'Process' is the methodology employed in using the various products available to library media specialists and teachers by which information and data may be obtained, analyzed, and used to solve learning problems.

Educational needs are varied

Principle 7 of the Learning and Teaching Principles for school library media programs refers to 'diverse learning abilities, styles, and needs' of the 'learning community'. This principle acknowledges that different groups have different needs, capabilities, and learning styles.

- The learning community may be regarded as a concentric ring of collaborative groups emanating outward from its center, the school library media program.
- Student needs, capabilities, and styles are distinct from those of outlying groups. The library media program must be able to accommodate learning styles, disabilities, and curriculum objectives set down by teachers, administrators, library specialists, and state educational components.
- School administrators have need of measurement and assessment technology of school academic programs designed to augment information literacy of today's students.
- Professional associations like the AASL seek and disseminate information regarding new technologies and learning research.

Professional learning community

The most current model for a 'professional learning community' is the model established by the AASL (American Association of School Librarians)

Copyright © Mometrix Media. You have been licensed one copy of this document for personal use only. Any other reproduction or redistribution is strictly prohibited. All rights reserved.

Like other information professional communities, it consists of a network of library media specialists and teachers who exchange ideas, methods, and other communication by all means including use of the internet.   Modern professional learning communities like AASL make use of web-conferencing, conventional protocols like email and ftp (a file sharing protocol which allows transmission of large files over the internet) to share documents. Live chat lines are established in order to provide technical advice and assist on information literacy problems. Also shared are useful links to information, criticism and commentary on new developments.

Jean Piaget

Jean Piaget is known for his four stages of child cognitive development.   The four stages of Piaget's cognitive development theory are:

- Sensorimotor Development: A period of time up to age 2, according to Piaget. During this time, the child learns and functions largely through sensual stimuli.
- Preoperations Stage: Spans the period of time from age 2 to age 6. The most important change in child development that occurs at this stage is the ability to conceptualize and to perceive objects outside of the range of the child's self-centered existence.
- Concrete operations' is a stage of learning development which occurs between the ages of seven through eleven. The child becomes increasingly logical, more systematic, learns to count without visual aids.
- Piaget's fourth stage of development is called 'formal operations', a period of time when the child begins to operate within the full scale of human reasoning.

Copyright © Mometrix Media. You have been licensed one copy of this document for personal use only. Any other reproduction or redistribution is strictly prohibited. All rights reserved.

Synchronous and asynchronous instruction

The differences between the two types of instruction is in the span of time during which learning content is delivered.

- Synchronous Learning occurs in 'real time', is interactive. Communication passes in two directions. Audio and video streaming on 'live' websites are examples of 'synchronous' instruction delivered via internet. Many young people are accustomed to 'chat', another kind of synchronous communication via internet. Web conferencing and Voice over IP are additional examples and allow for the learner to communicate with the teacher or LMS.
- Examples of Asynchronous technology consist of CD-ROMS, DVDs, multimedia clips, blogs. The information may be extensive, but it is 'static.' The user of such information is limited in communication and in the resolution of learning problems. Communication in this manner is a one-way road.

Learning styles

Learning styles are diverse and teachers who are familiar with the various types have a greater chance of success.

- Verbal or Linguistic learning styles are preferred by learners who learn best by reading and writing and by oral presentation of material by a teacher.
- Visual-Spatial learners make great use of charts, maps, diagrams, or other methods in which ideas and content can be conveyed visually.
- Kinesthetic Learning is judged best for the type of learner who needs to be doing an activity in order to learn it. The 'learn-by-doing' teaching technique is one which is interactive and allows physical movement to demonstrate educational content.
- Intrapersonal Learning works best with the reflective individual. The interpersonal learner tends to relate educational content to how she/he feels about it. Reflection and quiet analysis are typical learning strategies for the interpersonal learner.

Teaching strategies

Different teaching stratagems may be designed and directed toward different learners:

- An intrapersonal learner is a person who likes to reflect on learning tasks and review them internally. This person tends to categorize and organize things in terms of their feelings. A good teaching strategy which advantages the reflective or interpersonal learner would be an assignment to keep a journal or diary.
- The Verbal-Linguistic learner does well with traditional teaching techniques which employ books, magazine articles, or online print sources.
- The Bodily or Kinesthetic Learner might learn best using a video game requiring physical movement as the type of interaction with instructional content. Interactive simulations are a good teaching strategy for this type of learner. This technique is often used in military and police training.
- Visual-Spatial learners might respond well to certain web-based presentations which require object analysis and examination, or by the use of three-dimensional modeling.

Web tutorial design concepts

There are certain common elements in successful web-based learning activities:

Copyright © Mometrix Media. You have been licensed one copy of this document for personal use only. Any other reproduction or redistribution is strictly prohibited. All rights reserved.

- Be clear about your objectives. Define your purpose, and the target audience.
- Provide for different types of learners. Design the material accordingly.
- Organize content by concept rather than by a single item designation. An entire group of learning activities should be organized around a single concept or idea.
- Use contemporary language and topic examples. Make the subject entertaining but don't bury the content by making entertainment value the sole objective.
- Web-based Tutorials should always have a reference link which will allow contact with an education professional, usually an LMS or a Nationally Board Certified Teacher.

Bandwidth and plug-ins

Library Specialists and National Board Certified Teachers function in an increasingly technological world. They will have to answer many questions which arise from the use of technology in computer-based instruction or in the teaching of information literacy.

- Bandwidth is a term related to the amount of data which can be passed through from the internet to the end user and the speed at which it can move. Today's multimedia requires large bandwidth. Library hardware choices must reflect an awareness of the need to fit large amounts of data through the information 'pipeline'.
- Plug-ins are small applications which must be installed on a computer in order to view specific types of content. Certain content providers and application developers require 'plug-ins' (Java or Adobe PDF formats, for example) to function properly. The LMS must know when installation of a plug-in is appropriate and anticipate the learner's questions about 'plug-in' messages which crop up on the computer screen.

Script language

Programming languages which operate computer applications can be highly specialized and difficult. However, there are several programming languages called 'script' languages which are intentionally less complicated and designed primarily for the purpose of web page design. It is important for the LMS and other educators to be aware of the most commonly used of these 'script 'languages as they are frequently encountered in web-based instruction and other content.

- Active-X was developed by Microsoft. It can be downloaded for free and is needed to view some web content.
- Java is another common script language. It was developed by Sun Microsystems, and designed to be platform independent. That means it doesn't need the Windows operating system to work. Its basic functions can be downloaded for free.

Influences of behaviorist psychology

The behaviorist school of psychology had a powerful early impact on educational psychology. While some of behaviorist's mechanistic theories have been rejected by modern educators, it's most relevant precepts continue to be a part of learning and of information literacy. The influence of the behaviorists is apparent in online and offline tutorials. The following behaviorist concepts continue to be part of modern educational theory.

- Reinforcement and feedback must be part of the learning process.
- Reinforcement of learning progression will help students to learn at a more rapid pace.
- Active participation is crucial to learning.
- Learners should be allowed to work at their own pace.

Copyright © Mometrix Media. You have been licensed one copy of this document for personal use only. Any other reproduction or redistribution is strictly prohibited. All rights reserved.

Levels of Competence

The NBPTS Four Levels of Competence refer to a progression of learned standards experienced by teachers/ media specialists.
- Stage 1 - Refers to a level called 'unconscious incompetence'. Within this context, the individual is functioning in a sort of vacuum and is unaware of an outside body of knowledge which is essential to learning progress.
- Stage 2 - Refers to the level called 'conscious incompetence'. The difference here is that the individual becomes aware of a body of knowledge outside the realm of his/her own functioning, but is not capable of implementing appropriate achievement strategies.
- Stage 3 - This is the level of 'conscious competence' in which the individual is both conscious and active in achievement of large group task objectives.
- Stage 4 – Called 'unconscious competence', this refers to the most complete level of understanding and performance. The learning process is so ingrained that it emerges without conscious effort.

NBPTS certification process

The NBPTS writing test has three components: description, analysis, and reflection.
- Description: The candidate is given a task to develop within the context of a scene, objective and setting. The candidate must address the problem, reveal strategies for instruction which indicate a deep level of awareness and competence in description, and provide convincing evidence of high competency teaching standards.
- Analysis: Just as you might think, analysis refers to the part of the NBPTS writing exam where the candidate assesses the various parts of the learning task. Which parts could have been done better? Which strategies and techniques worked? Were the objectives of the lesson attained?
- Reflection: While 'reflection' can be considered part of analysis, the NBPTS exam looks at reflection as a category apart. The idea is to take analysis to a new level, expanding it beyond the physical components described during the 'analysis' component.

Co-planning

The NBPTS uses the term 'co-planning' to mean that planning is coordinated between the library media specialist and the classroom teacher from the inception of the learning plan. The NBPTS makes the distinction that 'adding on' a unit of information literacy to a classroom teacher's plan is not co-planning. The idea behind co-planning is that the classroom teacher and the media specialist must initially design the lesson plan with a view toward both curriculum objectives and information literacy at the same time. The integration is done while the learning strategy is being developed, not afterward. This means that neither partner in the co-planning exercise should dominate the process nor have pre-existent ideas of how the combination of information literacy and content learning can be integrated.

Power relationships

The NBPTS describes three types of 'power' relationships which can impact collaboration between classroom teacher and library media specialist.

Copyright © Mometrix Media. You have been licensed one copy of this document for personal use only. Any other reproduction or redistribution is strictly prohibited. All rights reserved.

- Royalty vs. Lowly Subject Relationship: In this scenario, the library media specialist is a reigning monarch while the library is the kingdom. The 'lowly subject' (the classroom teacher) cannot enter with classes without acceding to the Supreme Ruler of the domain. This is an unequal relationship which impedes achievement of educational goals.
- Professional vs. Client Relationship: In this scenario, the library media specialist is cast in the role of doctor, lawyer, CEO, fitting the classroom teacher into the schedule grudgingly. The effect of making everyone uncomfortable is a detriment to information literacy.
- Friend-To-Friend Relationship: This is a relationship where power is equally balanced between the classroom teacher and the library media specialist. Both parties are open to the development of strategies, and both are open to revisions. Flexibility is necessary in this most desirable power relationship.

Copyright © Mometrix Media. You have been licensed one copy of this document for personal use only.
Any other reproduction or redistribution is strictly prohibited. All rights reserved.

Co-planning sessions

There are certain steps which the LMS must undertake prior to meeting with the classroom teacher in a co-planning session.

- The LMS must become entirely familiar with the curriculum lesson in the subject area. Knowing that an eighth grade Language Arts program contains a unit or block on researching and writing a report on a menu of listed topics is an important first step.
- An examination of topic listings before meeting with the classroom teacher is essential.
- Knowing in advance what information can be researched and what means can be use in the media center is also of vital importance to a co-planning session. Since library collections are always in the process of being updated and revised, the classroom teacher may not be aware of all resources available for the project. The LMS should be prepared to advise and provide assistance in this area.

Co-teaching strategies

Assistive teaching, Support, Parallel, Alternative, and Team teaching are five methods outlined by Friend and Cook.

- Assistive teaching is a co-teaching method in which the library media specialist is in a helping role and responds to the classroom teacher's leadership.
- Parallel teaching is a structure that physically divides the classroom.
- Support teaching is a type of assistive teaching but the difference is that the support teacher usually follows the path of selected students. A library information literacy session might consist of classroom teacher, support teacher, and the LMS.
- Alternative teaching has the classroom divided by topic. The LMS may work with students on organization in the media center while the teacher remains in the classroom with other students learning another topical content area.
- Team teaching means that both teacher and LMS serve roles that are determined by the content area and curriculum. Both members of the team are in the same space.

Using traditional books

Books in the media center/library should be collected with a view toward advancing the curriculum objectives. There are many fiction books which lend themselves to Language Arts study. It must be noted, however, that many titles lend themselves very well to usage in various content areas, be it history or science.

Elementary school Science or Geography curricula might advantageously use Judi Barrett's Cloudy with a Chance of Meatballs for a weather study unit, for example.

A History lesson might well use My Brother Sam Is Dead as a fiction work with powerful historical underpinnings. That book very well highlights the conditions and divergent loyalties of various groups during the American Revolution.

Purpose of videotaping

A National Board Certified Teacher candidate is expected to provide videotapes as part of the portfolio used to assess NBCT performance. It behooves the candidate to make frequent videotapes, and then select the ones that reflect progress toward professional teaching standards.

Copyright © Mometrix Media. You have been licensed one copy of this document for personal use only. Any other reproduction or redistribution is strictly prohibited. All rights reserved.

The best videotape to use in the portfolio is not one that is 'picture perfect' since that rarely happens in the classroom environment. It's more important to have a video example which shows how the candidate deals with chance classroom occurrences and interruptions, as well as videotape which shows the progress of selected students. The NBCT assessor will not be judging the candidates videotape on production values, nor on hairstyles, but will focus on growth and depth of understanding.

Assessing research information

When students conduct library research, they must learn how to organize the materials they discover in terms of importance and relevancy. A 'hand-out' can initially be given to students which require them to utilize certain tools in evaluating data.

- Purpose - Does the item contribute to the purpose (or report) for which the information is to be used? Does it detract? Is there more relevant information?
- Audience - Is the data retrieved suitable for the audience? Is it too basic? Too technical for the target audience?
- Accuracy - Assess accuracy by using backup sources. Does all the data lead to the same conclusion? Is some of the data at variance with other data?

Authoritative sources

One of the primary things to consider when assessing information is whether the information comes from an authoritative source. A source may be accurate but not always authoritative. Authoritative sources are those that are accepted widely because they follow an intense verification protocol. Facts will be checked again and again. A newspaper like the Wall Street Journal is an authoritative source when providing information about certain financial activity. When a source like the Wall Street Journal publishes items in a subjective, non-factual area, it will identify subject information as such. An example of an accurate source which is not authoritative is the Wikipedia website. While Wikipedia encompasses vast information resources, and while the content may be completely accurate, the data is compiled by users of varying and often disputed degrees of expertise.

Primary and secondary sources

The differences between primary and secondary information is often confused by students and adults alike. This blurring occurs because very often a source is perceived to be 'authoritative' because it is widely recognized and experienced. Yet this 'authoritative' and widely recognized source may be routinely generating information obtained from secondary sources.

Responsible news organizations try their utmost to inform their audiences of their use of secondary sources, yet because something is written in Time or Newsweek magazine, it is often repeated (and used by students) as a primary source.

Copyright © Mometrix Media. You have been licensed one copy of this document for personal use only. Any other reproduction or redistribution is strictly prohibited. All rights reserved.

A true primary source is direct. Consider an ABC News broadcast of a Gallup poll stating that '....according to a recent Gallup poll, a majority of people believe that global warming was invented by Al Gore'. Verbatim repetition of the ABC broadcast would be using a secondary source of information. Using a primary source would be to present the actual poll for all to see, read, and interpret.

Subjective and objective sources

Subjective sources are those that reflect the personal logical and emotional point of view of the information provider. Common examples are the newspaper editorial and letters to the editor.

Very clever presenters of information intentionally blur the lines between real facts and subjective information. This is termed 'persuasive' writing and it is commonly found in newspaper columns and editorials.

Objective sources of information are derived from direct experimentation. Real facts are often at variance with subjective material. A scientific research report which has been repeated many times with the same result is a good example of objective material. Another example of objective material would be the product specifications of an appliance brochure where the information is obtained by scientific measurement.

Using commercial websites

A dot.com URL extension is a clear indication that the purpose of a website is to make money.   It is of utmost important that media specialists and classroom teachers inform students how to evaluate dot.coms on the internet.

An important consideration should be to determine the target goals and target audience of the site. Sometimes these are stated, sometimes not. Many commercial services provide accurate, up-to-date and reliable information for a subscription fee. Lexis-Nexis is just one example of one such subscription fee service.   It is often purchased by academic and law libraries. Indeed, much of what appears on a library computer's menu of databases is purchased from commercial companies, including the internet connection itself. There are Dow Jones information services which can be purchased for specialized financial information and research. Such companies may be said to be in the information business and have a good record of reliability.

Evaluating website credibility

The LMS-Teacher familiarizes students with criteria for evaluation of the credibility of a website authored by an individual or group of individuals. After ascertaining the purpose of the website, the student should focus on the following:
- Can the author(s) of the site be identified or is there an attempt to provide information anonymously?
- Does the website producer vouch for the accuracy of the content?
- Does the website provide contact access through physical and online addresses?
- Do the producers of the website provide resumes of their author(s), including education, experience and position?
- Is the content itself believable?

Copyright © Mometrix Media. You have been licensed one copy of this document for personal use only. Any other reproduction or redistribution is strictly prohibited. All rights reserved.

- Does the author-producer have an affiliation with a commercial company, an academic institution, or a non-profit organization?

Website accuracy evaluation

The LMS-Teacher should familiarize student with the various means of evaluating the accuracy of information obtained from websites. While some of this is the same criteria used to evaluated print sources, there a tendency among students to believe information which comes from multimedia internet sources.

- Does the website reference information sources from which the information is derived?
- Does the website clearly 'tag' or identify statistical data in a clear and comprehensible method of organization?
- Does the website provide corroborating information or links to better-known and widely accepted reliable information sources?
- Do the links connect the user to the stated website link or does it attempt to divert the user to other irrelevant content areas?
- Does the website use correct grammatical structures? Does it have spelling, or typographical errors? These are clues to reliability and accuracy.

Copyright © Mometrix Media. You have been licensed one copy of this document for personal use only. Any other reproduction or redistribution is strictly prohibited. All rights reserved.

Timeliness of website information

The information seeking student may look to the following clues in determining the timeliness of information on a website:

- Websites providing information often date the material being offered. Most often, the algorithms of the search engine will provide this information, just as a newspaper publishes the date of each issue.
- Has the information been updated? Just as many textbooks are published in first, second, and third revised editions (depending on popularity and relevance), so should websites update information to reflect change.
- The prevalence of 'dead' links are a clue that a website has been abandoned or orphaned by the developer. In the quick-changing world of web production and design, the presence of a single dead link does not mean the entire website is unreliable, but a profusion of 'dead' links is a strong indicator that the website is out of date.

Objective or subjective sources

To assess the objectivity or bias of a website, the information literate student should consider the following questions:

- Does the site offer a single opinion or point of view? Does it offer a variety of opinions on the same subject? Does it present the 'other side' of an issue? This is of particular importance in assessing the bias of a news organization, advocacy group, or a 'blog'.
- Does the site finance itself through advertising, by subscription, or by contributions? Who are the financiers behind the website? Is it supported by a single person with out-of-pocket expenditures? All of these things will impact the objectivity of information provided on a website.
- Does the stated objective or mission correspond with the type of business engaged in by the company which sponsors it? Is there a parent corporation responsible for content?
- Being able to assess the objectivity of information is of vital concern in an era of political controversy, change, and upheaval.

Application of fair use

The doctrine of 'fair use' is a legal term which defines the conditions under which the use of copyrighted material will not be considered an infringement of copyright law. 'Fair use' allows the use of copyrighted material for various purposes: teaching and scholarship activity, research, the reporting of news, and certain types of critical analysis. Use of the copyrighted material must not be such that it diminishes marketplace demand for the original, as would occur with the copying and distribution of books, film, CDs, and software. The person using the copyrighted material must not represent the material as his/her own.

Copyright © Mometrix Media. You have been licensed one copy of this document for personal use only. Any other reproduction or redistribution is strictly prohibited. All rights reserved.

Invisible Web

Internet searches consist of broadly available materials such as those which might be accessed with common search engines like Google or Yahoo or AltaVista. These are genera-purpose search engines and these lead to what one may call the visible web. However, there is an underlying network of less accessible sources called the 'Invisible Web'. These sources are not as easily accessed and some require a password. Others may be accessed but protected by 'firewalls' or other obstacles to entry. The 'invisible web' often contains a great deal of scholarly information of much better use to researchers than generalized sources. The more accessible of the invisible web sources are operated by educational and government agencies.

Meta-search Engine

Conventional search engines like Yahoo or Google have access to millions of catalogued web pages which can be displayed upon the request for information by a user. A meta-search engine is a way of querying a host of conventional search engines at the same time. The meta-search engine then compiles the results of all the searches and sends them to the user. The advantage of this type of search engine is speed; the disadvantage is that meta-search technologies do not penetrate to the fullest extent of the databases searched. Meta-search protocols stop searching after a number of results are obtained. Sometimes the meta-search query misses certain large and well-known database resources and returns no information.

Continuity in library funding

The Library Media Specialist must be active in insuring that the media center receives sufficient funding attention to maintain its collection. In order to do so:
- The LMS must understand the school budgeting process.
- The LMS must be aware of the timetable of the budget cycle and be sure that target dates are met. The LMS should interface with all persons who have input into the budget process to be sure that school officials are acting timely to move the library budget forward..
- The LMS must know who the key staff are, maintain connections with them, asking questions and resolving issues where appropriate.
- The LMS must insure that the needs of the library are clearly identified and made known to the appropriate personnel.

Budget plan components

The components of the media center budget plan should include the following items:
- A budget item for new resources should be a separate line item of the library budget. The LMS should communicate to others in the budgeting chain that facilities and materials must remain current.
- A budget item for promotional materials like posters and signs is needed to direct usage and encourage reading, as well as to inform users of library rules. Some libraries make rooms for displays depicting historical, scientific, and literary themes.
- Administrative materials like paper, printer ink, staples, copy toners and a host of other stationery supplies are a consistent budget item which should be proportionate to average monthly usage.

Copyright © Mometrix Media. You have been licensed one copy of this document for personal use only. Any other reproduction or redistribution is strictly prohibited. All rights reserved.

- An amount should be specified for promotional events involving the community, teachers, and the library media center.

Some items required but maybe not in the media budget:
- ICT (Information and Communications Technology) costs may or may not be included in the specific library budget. These costs are usually associated with software purchase or licensing costs.
- Staff costs are sometimes included directly in the library budget as a separate item, but in some schools, library staff is included in the general staff budget.
- The LMS should be aware of the budget method used in their library and should advocate for the appropriation of sufficient funds. Statistics show that students score higher on standardized tests when they come from schools with more library staff, more technology, periodicals or other materials. Statistical studies point to the same conclusion regardless of economic factors.

Budget size

Various organizations like the AASL recommend that a school library material budget should be approximately five percent of the expenditure per student of the entire school district. The recommended five percent figure does not include salaries of non-library staff, special education costs, transportation or school expansion or remodeling costs.

Another useful tool for the Library Media Specialist-Teacher is the annual budget report from previous years. Previous year budget reports may not be sufficient to achieve current media center and curriculum goals. Where a shortfall of funding is perceived, the Library Media Specialist-Teacher must convey this to school administration and budget prognosticators, emphasizing that successful library produce successful academic performance, according to existing studies.

Information literacy collaboration

Collaboration in teaching information literacy has many advantages:
- Collaboration increases the chance of student success. Having the classroom teacher and the library media specialist work together means better educated, information literate students.
- Collaboration requires the LMS to be an information literacy leader and not a mere housekeeper of media center materials.
- Collaboration contributes to the education and training of other staff. It also is a way for the LMS to get connected with the different teacher strategies for reaching district curriculum goals.
- Collaboration with classroom teachers provides a kind of insurance for the ethical use of information. When all parties of a collaborative effort are allied in a single purpose and are mutually aware of the potential for plagiarism or unethical use, the students profit through better use of information tools and methods of organization.

Role of the SLMS

It is important for the School Library Media Specialist to be available for consultation with other school staff, particularly classroom teachers. This does not mean doing the work of other staff, but collaborating with them, helping to keep them informed of technological developments and

Copyright © Mometrix Media. You have been licensed one copy of this document for personal use only.
Any other reproduction or redistribution is strictly prohibited. All rights reserved.

changes, and finding solutions for mutual curriculum problems. When you're consulting with a classroom teacher, information and knowledge flows in two directions. The spread of technology in information learning is an immense field and it is impossible to be aware of all aspects of it. However, the SLMS is a focal point, pulling together traditional resources and integrating them with new resources in information technology. Integration of technology with learning has high cost initial outlays, but once implemented, it can help you function within budget constraints.

Planning criteria

In planning a new school library, it is important to consider the location and flexibility of physical space. Location and flexibility of space may seem like obvious concerns, but they can have great impact on the media center functions.

- Central location - It's best for a school library to be on the ground floor of a multi-story building. It will provide easier access to suppliers, teachers, administrators, and students (especially those with physical limitations). Members of the community must be accommodated when their presence is warranted for special projects. Centrality to classrooms and teaching areas encourages and enables use of the library space and materials.
- Flexibility of space means that the planners have designed the library so that different groups and displays may be accommodated at the same time.

Physical design issues

When planning a new school media center, the planners must be mindful of:

- Noise and traffic patterns. Cafeterias are areas of frequent student movement, as is the gymnasium. Music or band activity can also be distracting.
- Appropriate lighting conditions must be created through the judicious placement of windows and artificial lighting. Lighting affects mood and behavior.
- Temperature conditions. Temperatures affect student and staff performance particularly in geographic areas where temperature extremes are common. Air-conditioning and balanced heating systems are expensive, but important.
- Design which accommodates special needs students is absolutely necessary.
- The library space should be designed with separate areas for study and research areas, information desks, and computer stations. It should have a separate teaching area large enough to accommodate a full classroom of students and allow room for LMS-Teacher.

School library collection

The size of a library can only be described in general terms. Much will depend upon the size of the students to be served, budgetary considerations, and curriculum goals. It is necessary for the LMS, however, to project a vision of that ideal library and its materials:

- A rough guideline for a reasonable collection in a mid-sized school is considered ten books per students.
- AASL and other organizations have recommended that approximately sixty percent of the book content should consist of non-fiction resources. The stock of books should be balanced to meet the needs of various age groups, cultures, and abilities.
- It is important for the school library to acquire materials which entertain and amuse students while providing information. Novels, music, computer games, and magazines encourage reading, learning, and information seeking.

Copyright © Mometrix Media. You have been licensed one copy of this document for personal use only. Any other reproduction or redistribution is strictly prohibited. All rights reserved.

Standardization of electronic resources

It is important that a library's electronic media and catalogues follow standardized formatting of bibliographic information.
- Conforming to AASL cataloguing standards will insure broad access and information sharing.
- Very often school libraries are linked to nearby community and outside-of-district school libraries to provide a wider array of information sources. In some cases, online bibliographies and catalogues have been combined into a single database source which can be accessed from remote locations.
- Standardization of online catalogues and databases contributes is the best way of reaching the diverse community of interests and cultures. When online information databases are constructed with regard to standards of efficiency and ease of use, learning is opened up to the widest possible audience.

Fundamental skills required

Some school library positions are specialized and require specific training and credentials. However, all library staff personnel must be capable of dealing with school administrators, parent groups, educational counselors, teachers, and even politicians.
- Library staff must demonstrate communication skills and knowledge of students and the community.
- The ability to communicate with children is essential, along with the ability to grasp user needs.
- Knowledge of literature for children and young adults is a basic requirement for all library staff.
- Cooperation is an important skill. Library staff must cooperate with all school department personnel and contingent offices.
- Understanding cultural diversity is an essential skill in teaching students how to use information.

Library funding sources

Public library funding sources are different from those associated with school libraries. School libraries are directly funded from school district budgets, though they may receive funding augmentation from outside sources.. Some common potential funding sources for public libraries are:
- County Taxes: Some communities apportion a small percentage of county taxes or municipal taxes to fund library operation.
- Library Foundations: Foundations are often set up for public library funding and rely on tax-free charitable contributions. Tax exemptions make this a more attractive form of funding in some areas.
- Private Grants: Private grants are a source of funding for some public libraries. Typically, private grants are offered by businesses and corporations who wish, for a variety of good reasons, to contribute to the communities in which they are established.

Copyright © Mometrix Media. You have been licensed one copy of this document for personal use only. Any other reproduction or redistribution is strictly prohibited. All rights reserved.

Assistive keyboard devices

An LMS must be aware of federal and state education grants available for the purchase of assistive devices for library use.   The ALA recommends that school library media centers reach out to all learning communities. One of the ways to do this is through the use of assistive devices. Many devices are available to insist in the inclusion of some learners to the curriculum of information literacy.   Two common assistive devices are:

- Large print, touch-pad, and one-handed keyboards. These are assistive to users with motor impairment, loss of limbs, or vision problems.
- Software magnifiers, Braille display, and wireless audio connections are designed to assist the visually impaired. Some devices are designed to work in conjunction with standard PC and laptop configurations.

Copyright © Mometrix Media. You have been licensed one copy of this document for personal use only. Any other reproduction or redistribution is strictly prohibited. All rights reserved.

Braille Translators

There are several assistive devices designed for communication between teacher and student visual impairment. The Braille Translator has many variations:
- Products like Beginner Braille allow the teacher to customize a Mega-Dots learning program for different performance levels.
- Braille 2000 is a Braille Translator which enables a student to communicate over the internet. Communication by means of technology such as Braille 2000 can translate XML internet code to Braille signals. A demo version is available for free download so that prospective purchasers can review its capability.

LMS should look for compatibility with previously owned assistive devices and operating software when considering new purchases.

Assistive devices

Five assistive devices which can be used to extend learning access to all students include:
- TTY or TDD technology. This refers to a variety of device which allows communication with the hearing impaired. Incoming voice data is relayed to a center where words are translated into print and output to the hearing impaired person. The data then appears on a screen and can be read by the hearing impaired user.
- Voice recognition software. VR software has become sophisticated and can be used to direct software operation as well as to convert voice into text without typing.
- Flexible workstations can be adapted for use by persons who must remain in wheelchairs.
- Keyboarding is made easier for persons with certain limitations. Available keyboards include: touchscreen; one-handed keyboards; alternative keyboards which are designed around the specific limitation; large-print keyboards; and a large variety of trackballs and joysticks.

Literacy student assessments

The information literate student needs frequent evaluation and feedback relating to progress toward curriculum goals. Evaluation is needed as a measure of individual student growth.
- Assessment of the information literacy student is necessary to the improvement of media center teaching methods. When assessment shows less than desirable performance levels, the LMS can use performance measurement tools to determine the areas in need of revision.
- Testing and assessment recognizes individual student accomplishment. The feedback provided by testing can be used to inform the student and convey useful information to parents.
- Assessment can be used to determine the overall validity of the library media center program. Combined assessment of all classes conducted is a measurement criterion of overall library performance.

Tools of assessment

Forms can be set up online and put to a variety of evaluative uses.
- Online questionnaires are valuable tools for gathering opinions of students and obtaining input from other partners in the information literacy team. Online questionnaires and surveys are a good method of obtaining demographic information from students and

Copyright © Mometrix Media. You have been licensed one copy of this document for personal use only. Any other reproduction or redistribution is strictly prohibited. All rights reserved.

other users. The LMS can use survey information to develop an overall knowledge of student computer skill levels, interests, and general knowledge.

- A major advantage of the use of forms is anonymity. Students who might not be willing to offer public opinions may be willing to respond anonymously to controlled questions on a survey or questionnaire.
- Information required by survey questions can be directed toward very specific areas.

Online forms advantages

Online assessment forms have certain advantages over paper forms.
- Owing to the popularity of computer game technology, students are accustomed to getting feedback on individual performance levels. Performance levels are fundamental and basic to nearly all game technology. In the library media center, this translates to an opportunity for self-assessment.
- Interactive forms designed expressly for this purpose may programmed easily toward accepting input from students and providing immediate feedback. Correct responses lead the student to subsequent questions and levels. Interactive learning programs can eliminate learning anxiety for students when they know that 'feedback' (response to incorrect answers) is relayed back only to the learner and not to the teacher or LMS. This enables the learner to move ahead at a pace which befits that particular individual.
- Interactive forms can also be used for formal testing where response is checked for accuracy and given a grade.

Student assessment criteria

Student assessment methods should meet certain criteria:
- Assessment should measure what it is designed to measure.
- The scoring methods of a test should be clearly defined, and directly related to national standards, and the curriculum objectives of the school district.
- Assessment should be designed with specific levels of competence which can be clearly defined and demonstrated.
- It's important also that the method of assessment be challenging enough to exercise the faculties of the students.
- Student assessment should have real-world relevance. A testing strategy that does not encompass real-world challenges is not a valid measure of student success.

Language arts collaboration

A collaboration between a classroom Language Arts teacher and the school media specialist might take the following form:
- The Language Arts teacher conducts a month-long unit on research and writing upon each of four topics.
- The Language Arts teacher and the LMS arrange to discuss the project over lunch. .
- The Language Arts teacher and the LMS develop the project objectives: development of writing skills, better research through information literacy.
- They meet several times during the week to work out a library schedule and a method of splitting the classroom groups into two. The LMS and the Language Arts teacher arrange

Copyright © Mometrix Media. You have been licensed one copy of this document for personal use only. Any other reproduction or redistribution is strictly prohibited. All rights reserved.

to provide instruction on print and online search techniques, reinforcing the manner in bibliographic references are to be annotated.

- The LMS pulls up a list of books and materials from the computer terminal and directs the library staff to assemble the materials in the specific locations for better access.

Using statistics

Statistics are generally used a method of predicting future behaviors or trends. Statistical data may come from a variety of sources.

The U.S. government is a large collector of statistics. An example of the various government bureaus which provide statistics are: the Census Bureau; the Bureau of Economic Analysis, the Bureau of Labor Statistics, the National Center for Education Statistics, the Bureau of Justice Statistics, the national Center for Health Statistics, and the Bureau of Transportation Statistics. When trying to locate statistical informational, the first thing to do is to determine what kind of agency would need to collect the information.

Evaluate statistics on the basis of source, timeliness, potential for bias, and relevance to the information objective.

Problem-solving and thinking

Three concepts related to problem-solving and thinking are:
- Construction of Knowledge: Desirable learning models require students to develop new meanings and understanding rather than to memorize and repeat static information. Information without meaning or comprehension is of little use and will soon be forgotten.
- Disciplined Inquiry: This is a theory of learning which emphasizes the relationship between component data. Disciplined inquiry is directed toward solving problems. The collection of information fragments has little meaning in problem-solving unless they become integrated into learning schemata which help to resolve issues.
- Connections beyond School: This refers to the concept that schoolwork must have real-world application and meaning. Grades and academic success are not goals in themselves but are merely the tools and building blocks of real-world education.

Internet research advantages

The use of the internet for research has both advantages and disadvantages:
- Students should be informed that there is a great deal of useful information that isn't on the internet because it's not in digital form. Books, periodicals, and original documents are both necessary and fundamental to responsible research.
- There is no single reliable authority on the internet. It is collaboration between a wide variety of information and service providers, some of which are notoriously unreliable. Identifying reliable internet authorities should be one of the first concerns of internet users.
- The internet is a term used in the broadest sense of the word. The internet has sub-components like email, chat protocols, news bulletin boards, file transfer protocols, and a system of linked and individual web pages with a variety of purposes.

AIDS information sources

Copyright © Mometrix Media. You have been licensed one copy of this document for personal use only. Any other reproduction or redistribution is strictly prohibited. All rights reserved.

Four potential information sources where a student might find information on the topic of AIDS are:

- Magazines can be in the traditional printed form known as the 'periodical' or found online. Online magazines are called 'e-zines'. Magazines lend themselves to current and up-to-date information based on the periodical date of issue.
- Journals are written for specialized professional and academic fields. They may also be available online and called 'e-journals'.
- Index of Periodicals is a catalogue of periodicals and journals pertaining to particular subjects. They may contain excerpts from articles or full-text pieces.
- Newspapers are a fundamental source of information which are issued on a periodical or daily basis. Materials can be provided from primary or secondary sources.

Copyright © Mometrix Media. You have been licensed one copy of this document for personal use only. Any other reproduction or redistribution is strictly prohibited. All rights reserved.

'Dogs as Pets' information sources

Four information sources which may be used to gather data about this research topic are:

- Encyclopedias are a good source for this type of information. There are general and specific topic-directed types of encyclopedia. A general encyclopedia would be useful for research on this topic. Online encyclopedias are available by subscription.
- Books on dogs as pets are common in public and school libraries. Since it is an area of common experience, chances are good that you will find books on that subject widely available.
- A World Wide Web search would return thousands of entries on this topic. The task would be to find the relevant and useful ones and bypass sites which have purposes other than education information.
- The Library Catalog would be a good place to begin researching this topic. This will show the various items which are available in the school library collection.

Advantages of using library

There are advantages to using the resources of a library for research.

- One of the greatest advantages is that the researcher has the expertise of the library staff available for consultation purposes.
- The library staff has already organized the materials in a way that can be more easily used and accessed.
- Materials which become part of the library collection have been researched for relevance and for reliability. This filtering process would otherwise fall upon the shoulders of the individual researcher.
- It is a great advantage, too, that libraries contain older information which cannot be easily obtained, as well as current resources. Older books are often out of print and cannot be located without using the library collection or perhaps through the inter-library loan system.

Magazines versus scholarly journals

There are many differences between popular magazines and scholarly journals:

- Scholarly articles present information that is far more in depth than that provided in popular magazines. Popular magazines specialize in instant and general information which can quickly be ingested.
- Scholarly journals focus on empirical research studies. Popular magazines may cite 'research statistics' but these are second-hand sources. Journals may provide access to actual experimentation.
- Journals provide bibliographies; popular magazines do not. Bibliographies are important when seeking information because one can verify the information at the source.
- Journals are not supported by advertising. They are usually sponsored by professional or academic organizations. Hence, they do not have advertising, nor advertising camouflaged as news. Popular magazines display as much advertising as they can obtain from sponsors. While this is not necessarily bad, the amount of ad space sometimes dominates and diminishes the information content.

Computer information search

Copyright © Mometrix Media. You have been licensed one copy of this document for personal use only. Any other reproduction or redistribution is strictly prohibited. All rights reserved.

Many students take advantage of web searches such as those on the well-known search engines like Yahoo and Google. These search engines operate on the basis of Boolean logic. Even the cataloguing systems of libraries (OPACs) are structured in some form of logic for easier access. A major problem for students conducting information searches is that the techniques they use are too general. Information literate students must be taught how to expand and narrow their searches to get relevant search results.

- Students should be taught to refine search strategies before beginning the actual search. Jot down words, ideas, and concepts in advance.
- Students should examine the topic thoroughly and pick out the keywords which are important to the topic.
- Students should subject keywords to both narrowing and expansion, as there are times when search results must be narrowed and other times when they must be expanded. A knowledge of Boolean operators and sequencing protocols would be helpful.

'Computer email security' search

To conduct a sample search on the topic of 'computer email security':
- Make a few short sentences using the words 'computer security'.
- Jot down the keywords and key phrases in the sentences.
- Make a list of antonyms, synonyms, abbreviations, wider and narrower meanings for your words: electronic communications; e-mail; security software; encryption technology; phishing; website authentication; verification; etc...
- The library sources of information where you can find information on the topic.
- Combine search terms effectively and use search limiting strategies: Computers AND Security but NOT Security Guard*, for example.
- Narrow the general topics down to specifics.
- Now evaluate the credibility of the sources and select the information which originates from the most reliable sources. . Separate facts from opinion. Organize and identify secondary sources of credible information.

Library of Congress versus Dewey Decimal

A Library of Congress Catalogue number might be:
- HQ 801 G95 1998.
- HQ: Library of Congress call numbers begin with from one to three letters. These letters follow an alphabetical format. HQ means Sociology.
- 801: This number refers to the category of male-female relationships. Follows regular consecutive number sequence.
- G95: The 'G' represents the first letter of the author's last name. The numbers after the 'G' also follow a number sequence.

Dewey Decimal System: A typical designation in this system would be 306.70285 G994 058.
- First three numbers: 300s refer to the Social Sciences.
- Numbers after the decimal: Refer to 'relationships'.
- G994: refers to the author's last name in an alphabetic organization.
- 058: Refers to the title of the book.

Government information on Web

Copyright © Mometrix Media. You have been licensed one copy of this document for personal use only. Any other reproduction or redistribution is strictly prohibited. All rights reserved.

Searching federal government databases can be aided by knowledge of the following:

- Think of governmental structure. Get a diagram of the various government branches from a history or social studies book which shows the agencies which fall under the main three bodies of the government. Ask yourself if the information you seek could be found in the executive branch, the legislative branch, or the judicial branch.
- Start at the Executive Branch and the Office of the President. There the student will see active links to various agencies associated with the executive branch. There will also be links to the other branches of government.
- Use one of the well-known search engines to locate the URL of the agency. For example, a student should input 'U.S. Department of Education' to find the website of that government agency. The search link will have an internet extension of *.gov.

Public advocacy activities

Aside from setting up the library for use by a diverse population, the LMS should establish ongoing programs which contribute to interaction between the library, students, parents, and outside volunteers. The following activities are examples of things the LMS may do in the area of public advocacy:

- Conduct a Stuffed Animal Read-In for elementary school students. Children will bring their favorite stuffed animal to school. Volunteers will read associated children's literature. Send out press releases to newspapers and tv stations to inform others of the event.
- Form an Adventure Book Club. Locate materials associated with science, biology, and the outdoors. Interface with outdoor public conservation groups like the National Park Service to conduct field trips and other ancillary activity.

An advocacy program in the school library establishes a favorable relationship with the community outside the school. The purpose of advocacy is to form collaborative partnerships and other connections. Information literacy must extend to the community; it is not an isolated activity and does not happen in a vacuum. Other professionals and other learning communities can be linked by an active public advocacy program.

Public advocacy attracts attention to important causes and library needs. It's the library's job to make information needs a part of the public agenda. Public advocacy can be extended through the school newsletters, through displays, and through press releases.

Collaboration in advocacy

Collaboration in advocacy can be broken down into three components: Teachers, students, and the outside community.

- Teacher Collaboration: Motivate teachers in your school. If you are trying to focus attention on intellectual freedom, you must raise the issue in their content areas. Teachers are most likely to collaborate with the LMS when the advocacy program at the library focuses upon intellectual freedom in all areas: science, social studies, language arts, and music.
- Student Collaboration: Motivate the students to produce posters, newsletters, and to participate in a 'book review' contest. Students are the most energetic promoters the LMS will find. The trick is to motivate them.

Copyright © Mometrix Media. You have been licensed one copy of this document for personal use only. Any other reproduction or redistribution is strictly prohibited. All rights reserved.

- Community Collaboration: Assemble a group of volunteers for your reading program. Bring in speakers from the local historical society, nearby museums and public service organizations. Don't exclude the human resources at the public library.

Full-time librarians

Studies are ongoing in various states but statistics from completed studies in sixteen states are unanimous in showing that library media specialists trained as teachers have led to better performance scores on state achievement tests.

- Sixteen states have conducted research studies showing higher student achievement scores as the result of higher performance standards in information literacy.
- The experienced school library media specialist who excels in information access and library administration is a strong predictor of student achievement.
- A school with a certified library media specialist employed full-time is more likely to have collaborative connections to other schools, other professional resources, and the public library.
- Certified teacher-librarians in many schools have been able to secure more outside funding and to provide more instruction in the area of information literacy.

Copyright © Mometrix Media. You have been licensed one copy of this document for personal use only. Any other reproduction or redistribution is strictly prohibited. All rights reserved.

Raising achievement test scores

The library media center can help to raise student performance through:
- Flexible scheduling of library media center activities and hours.
- Adequate staffing consisting of at least one full-time teacher trained media specialist and sufficient support staff.
- Better funding and larger and more varied collections including electronic resources and connection and access to online resources.
- Encouragement and instruction of students in information literacy both as individuals and in collaborative groups.
- Giving students practice in the information literacy skills they need to make progress toward curriculum goals and by setting patterns of information seeking which will establish them as life-long learners.

According to a 2003 study in Illinois indicates that better student performance is linked most clearly to effective school library programs rather than socio-economic factors or spending per student.

Flexible scheduling

Flexible scheduling is one of the goals of an effective information literacy library teaching program. How the LMS and staff budget their time can determine the extent to which the library is used to further curriculum goals.

Flexible scheduling is difficult for library media specialists in schools where established policy is set and rigid for classroom teachers. Another impediment is that teachers are often so harried that they hesitate to take time necessary for collaboration with library staff. In this case, flexibility in scheduling is even more important. The LMS might have to rely on electronic communication and the telephone for collaborative efforts during school time, or extend services beyond the regular operating hours.

Very often the LMS might have to advocate for greater flexibility in scheduling and collaboration by making the case to teachers and administrative staff. Showing the statistics on overall school improvement based on productive collaboration with the school library is a good starting place to implement flexible scheduling.

Loertcher's theory

A balanced collection of materials which equally represents all fields is not a good model to follow for meeting curriculum goals. Loertcher recommends:
- A collection accurately focused on specific curriculum goals and weighted accordingly.
- A valid library collection methodology which considers and utilizes the expertise and selection experience of teachers in their subject fields.
- A library budget set from the information needs growing from high standards and principles of information literacy.
- Support, enhancement, or revision of the library collection in accordance with the curriculum objectives defined by the collaborative educational community.

Using adult fiction

Copyright © Mometrix Media. You have been licensed one copy of this document for personal use only. Any other reproduction or redistribution is strictly prohibited. All rights reserved.

Children can learn to perceive chronological development from the right choice of young adult fiction. Children strongly identify with character, family, and human situation when suitable books are used to develop learning about such topics as the American Revolution or other tales of the Colonial Era.

- Young adult fiction brings historical events to life in a way children can relate to in terms of community, religion, art, food and cultures.
- Historical timelines in fiction translate to an understanding of the student's individual personal timeline.
- Historical titles for young adults introduce them into the world of diverse political and social opinions, and acquaint them with fundamental principles of democracy.

Fundamentals of budgeting

School library operating budgets have typically been developed from four elements: information format, services, circulation or curriculum.

Criticisms can be made of each and most do not allow the degree of flexibility required to have a successful program. A budget based on 'information format' may not allow the LMS to shift dollars to meet student learning needs. A budget based on services provided leaves the various components competing with each other for dollars. The evaluation of use patterns is important information for the LMS to have but should not be used as a basis for budgeting as it may not increase student achievement.

A more realistic survey of the school library needs will examine the needs of the learner and drive the budget process.

Content standards and diversity

Students given instruction in information literacy should reach toward the following goals:

- Students should know the varieties of diversity their local communities as well as in the country at large.
- Students should understand how diversity contributes to cultural creativity.
- Student should understand and be able to write about and explain American conflicts which have developed due to conflicts generated by a diversity of population.
- Students should be able to explain and write about the manner in which conflicts can be peacefully resolved in a manner that respects individual rights and different cultures.
- Students should be well versed in the concept of the American identity, and that being an American means a belief in shared political values and community well-being regardless of cultural differences. They should be able to compare American values of diversity with other countries whose identity is based on narrower allegiances to singular ethnicities and religion.

Information Literacy Standards

The ALA's nine information literacy standards are broken down into three main categories: information literacy; independent learning; and social responsibility. There are three standards the student must meet in each of these three categories.

- Information Literacy refers to the treatment of information obtained from research and reading. How the student accesses and uses information is another part of this component.

Copyright © Mometrix Media. You have been licensed one copy of this document for personal use only. Any other reproduction or redistribution is strictly prohibited. All rights reserved.

- Independent Learning refers to the ability of a student to adapt information into the personal sphere. Independent learning leads to an appreciation of literature and other forms of information expression.
- Social Responsibility has special meaning within the nine ALA standards of information literacy for student learning. The three standards within this category refer to the student's awareness of his/her place in the learning community. Social Responsibility also means that the student recognizes the importance of accurate and truthful information in a democracy.

Information literacy standards

Three information standards of information literacy are:
- Standard One refers to the efficient use and access of information. In order to meet this standard, the student would be able to obtain, prioritize, and organize information, applying it to research and curriculum goals.
- Standard Two refers the ability to evaluate the information accessed. The student who meets this standard would be expected to use critical judgment in analyzing the value and accuracy of the information obtained.
- Standard Three refers to the use of information in ways that are both creative and viable. To meet this standard, the student would be able to apply organized information to a larger task in a way that is creative and leads to new developments and revelations.

Independent learning

Independent Learning is one of the nine Information Literacy Standards for Student Learning. It defines the goals of the information literate student in three areas:
- Standard 4: The student is information literate and able to independently pursue natural inclinations toward learning.
- Standard 5: The information literate student acquires the means to access and organize the volumes of information into a coherent body of knowledge. Students meeting this standard will be able to appreciate literature and the flow of ideas through all means of creative expression.
- Standard 6: Information literacy is the basic requirement of standard 6, but the standard is extended into a greater level of competence in data retrieval and collection. The student meeting Standard 6 is able to generate knowledge which overflows and transcends simple data.

Social responsibility

As ALA defines the standards for student learning, information literacy refers to the responsible use of information and knowledge.
- Standard 7: Within this context, the student is cognizant of his standing and role within the larger society and recognizes the importance of information to the preservation of democracy.
- Standard 8: The two important elements in this standard are the student's contribution to community and the habit of ethical behavior with regard to the use of information and the technology which delivers it.
- Standard 9: Students meeting this standard will contribute to the fund of knowledge in the large communities of learners. Aside from knowing how to access information

Copyright © Mometrix Media. You have been licensed one copy of this document for personal use only. Any other reproduction or redistribution is strictly prohibited. All rights reserved.

effectively, the student leads the community of learners in disseminating information as well as obtaining it.

Proficiency in information

The three levels of information literacy are to be found in each and every one of the nine standards for student learning. They are: basic, proficient, and exemplary. The level of functioning described by each level is incremental and variable.

- Basic: The student meeting the basic level of proficiency in Standard 1 is able to provide examples of when additional information is needed to resolve an issue or complete a task.
- Proficient: The student meeting the proficient level of Standard 1 for student learning recognizes the need to obtain information beyond the scope of his/her existing knowledge. The student has an understanding of those issues for which additional information is needed and knows where and how to obtain it.
- Exemplary: A student at the exemplary level of proficiency in Standard 1 will be able to assess whether a range of tasks or problems can be resolved through information gathering techniques.

Accurate and complete information

One of the indicators (Indicator 2) of the nine information literacy standards for student learning is that the student recognizes that accurate and complete information is necessary to the decision making process. Indicator 2 of Standard 1 also has three incremental levels of proficiency.

- The basic level for this indicator means the student is able to provide examples of both accurate and inaccurate information. The student also recognizes when information presents a partial picture or is complete.
- The proficient level for Indicator 2 of Standard 1 means the student is able to explain the deficiencies of information and can demonstrate how these deficiencies can lead to poor decision-making.
- The student who performs at an exemplary level of Indicator 2 is effective judge and analyst of information, able to discard faulty data and poorly grounded decision-making.

Framing questions

A third indicator of effective and efficient use of information as described in Standard 1 is that the student allows information needs to frame questions. Indicator 3 of Standard 1 also has three levels of proficiency.

- Basic: A student performing at this level will be able to formulate at least a single question which flows from his/her information needs.
- Proficient: At this level, the student will be able to define the problem broadly and in specific detail. The specificity will be an aid in finding the necessary information.
- Exemplary: This highest level of proficiency reflecting Indicator 3 means that the student is continuously revising information requests and questions to suit changing information needs.

Potential sources of information

Identifying potential sources of information is one of the indicators (Indicator 4) of Standard One of the Information Literacy Standards for Student Learning: accessing information efficiently and

Copyright © Mometrix Media. You have been licensed one copy of this document for personal use only. Any other reproduction or redistribution is strictly prohibited. All rights reserved.

effectively. The ALA defines three levels of proficiency in describing the traits exhibited by Indicator 4: Basic, proficient, and exemplary.

- The basic level of operation means that the student can list several information sources and knows what kind of information will be found in each. The student differentiates between newspaper and periodical, for example.
- The proficient level of operation means the student has an array of information sources available which can be accessed. The student approaches the task of sorting out this information by the process of brainstorming, noting ideas and potential problems in approach before extracting the information.
- Exemplary functioning is attained when the student uses and organizes the full potential of information gathering from all sources.

Graphic example

The topic example is the subject of genetically engineered crops like corn and soybeans.

- The teacher invites two classroom speakers. One of the speakers is from the state Department of Agriculture. The other is from a citizen organization opposed to genetically engineered crops.
- Students form in groups and schedule library time. While one group is in the library with the media specialist, others are brainstorming the topic.
- All groups assemble their information. Some students have found articles in newspapers and magazines. Another has found diagrams in a science book. Yet another has found numerous encyclopedia sources. Online sources are many but some of the students are uncertain about their reliability.
- The true leaders emerge. One of the students has found an online tutorial made in the research department of university which has an unusually clear animated film of the basic process. The teacher shows the animation to everyone. There is a class discussion, followed by the writing assignment.

Standard One required skills

Standard One of the NBPTS standards refers to Knowledge of Learners. 'Learners' is a very broad category which must be further defined.

- A 'learner' must be understood as a developing individual, that is, as one who progresses from infancy to adulthood and all the milestones in between. During the entire process, the 'learner' is acquiring new skills. Those skills and traits are best understood in the context of human growth and development, the various learning theories, and the differences between learners at various stages in their lives.
- The library media specialist must be able to work with students of all ages and abilities. Also important is the ability to recognize that certain individuals are inclined toward a particular learning style. Recognition of the various learning styles if elemental to attainment of the NBPTS Standard One, Knowledge of Learners.

Knowledge of learners influencers

Knowledge of Learners is an NBPTS standard based on the work of social scientists and educational theorists like Jean Piaget, Lev Vygotsky, and Benjamin Bloom. All of these scientists, in one way or another, emphasize the importance of social development in the process of learning. Knowledge of Learners is an important standard. It is important for teachers and librarian-teachers to recognize

Copyright © Mometrix Media. You have been licensed one copy of this document for personal use only. Any other reproduction or redistribution is strictly prohibited. All rights reserved.

the levels of functional development of students at varying ages. Bloom is noted for his 'taxonomy', a hierarchy of educational objectives which occur in sequence. Vygotsky emphasized that the cognitive development associated with learning was as much the result of social interaction and development as it was of academic content. Piaget is best remembered for this work in early childhood development. It is interesting to note that Piaget used his own children as the objects of study in developing his learning theories.

Levels of abstraction

Knowledge, Comprehension, Application, Analysis, Synthesis, and Evaluation are six levels of abstraction put forth by Benjamin Bloom in his taxonomy of educational development.

- Knowledge is first in Bloom's taxonomy. It means knowledge in its simplest form.
- Comprehension: The knowledge gains meaning and can be interpreted.
- Application: The basic or fundamental knowledge acquired can be applied to solve problems, to 'reason things through' for individual benefit.
- Analysis: This level of Bloom's taxonomy means that knowledge and its uses can be stripped down and perceived in its component parts.
- Synthesis: At the 'synthetic' level of education, the learner can analysis knowledge, disassemble it in the abstract, and recombine it to gain new insights and meanings.
- Evaluation: The learner can assess bodies of knowledge, can compare and discriminate between opposing and interlocking ideas.

Importance of Piaget's theories

Piaget's importance in the area of learning styles can be demonstrated by the activities of the early childhood education teacher. Piaget described several phases of child development during which learning occurs. The LMS or teacher must be fully aware of learning differences at different stages of development. Piaget describes the span of time from age two to age six of a child's development as a stage of 'pre-operation'. During this phase, the child begins to conceptualize outside objects. The higher functional state of 'concrete operations' does not occur until the child reaches age seven and continues to approximately age eleven. At that age, the child becomes increasingly logical, more systematic, learns to count without visual aids, and understands 'conservation', a key concept of Piaget's concrete operations stage. During Piaget's fourth stage of development the child can recognize the meaning of abstract concepts like 'truth' and 'justice'.

Building blocks of teaching

Capable teachers are familiar with the building blocks of solid teaching technique.

- Knowledge of learning theories is essential to the act of teaching.
- Delivery of instruction using a variety of methods is a function of teaching design. Classroom management, student testing, and curriculum development are all part of teaching design and instruction delivery technique.
- Pedagogical knowledge and principles are part of teaching. An effective teacher learns efficient and productive organizational skills, as well as various methods of communicating ideas orally and in writing. Effective instruction, whether from classroom teacher or LMS, is based on a thorough knowledge of the curriculum. Behavioral management is another part of pedagogy which is an essential skill in the classroom.

Copyright © Mometrix Media. You have been licensed one copy of this document for personal use only. Any other reproduction or redistribution is strictly prohibited. All rights reserved.

Library versus classroom

The NBPTS Knowledge of Teaching and Learning guidelines point out the differences of instructional delivery between two partners in collaboration, the library and the classroom.

- Behavioral management in the classroom is an ongoing process wherein the classroom teacher is able to devote more time to behavior management. The LMS does not have the advantage of prolonged attempts at behavior modifications. The classroom teacher, on the other hand, sees the students on a regular basis and can address issues which arise with certain individuals or groups. The LMS must 'get it right' the first time or risk losing valuable minutes which might be better used teaching information literacy.
- Another key difference is that the library media specialist functions in the role of an educational facilitator. While face-to-face instruction often does occur, it is likely that library time will be fast-paced and students will be embarked upon different paths of learning. The library media center is a multi-tasking environment and the LMS is the manager of that environment.

Standard Three of NBPTS

Knowledge of Library and Information studies includes but is not limited to the following library activities:

- Cataloguing and technical services for online materials and basic print materials is a fundamental requirement of the Library and Information Studies Standard Three.
- Management activities such as future planning and budget requirements.
- Evaluation and revision of library services and programs.
- Familiarization with literature, technology and information search skills.
- A basic understanding of hardware, software, and connectivity is also necessary to modern library information skills.
- Familiarity with researchers like Barbara Stripling, Carol Kuhlthau, and others is a vital component of functionality in the larger learning community. Common research methodologies like Big6 and I-search are routine in library information studies.

Diagnostic, formative, and summative assessments

Within the context of 'diagnostic' information skills assessment, Barbara Stripling points out the need to identify common misconceptions which students bring to the classroom when studying information literacy. Rooting out these misconceptions is part of her recommended diagnostic methodology, and must take place as additional learned is addressed.
Formative assessment techniques demand that teachers and library literacy instruction push students beyond levels of moderate skills acquisition. Barbara Stripling recommends various techniques to be used in 'formative assessment': Observation Checklists; Learning Logs; Rubrics, Concept Mapping, Exit Cards, and so forth.
Summative Assessment may be said to be a reformulation or remodeling of Bloom's taxonomy. Stripling uses the REACTS acronym to represent different levels of assessment: Recalling, Explaining, Analyzing, Challenging, Transforming, and Synthesizing.

NBCT required standards

The three standards and skill sets required to meet the requirements for a NBCT are the Integration of Instruction, Innovational Leadership, and Administration of the library media program.

Copyright © Mometrix Media. You have been licensed one copy of this document for personal use only. Any other reproduction or redistribution is strictly prohibited. All rights reserved.

Each of these skills is important in itself. Combined, these elements represent a set of skills which will make the library a central point in the instructional curriculum.

Curriculum requirements like Civics, Language Arts, Science or Mathematics cannot be taught as isolated disciplines without connection to information literacy. Each of the academic disciplines must be connected and interwoven with fabric of information awareness, analysis, and interpretation.

The Nationally Board Certified Teacher must lead the way in implementing this integration, reaching out to teachers in collaborative efforts, and directing the library's staff in meeting curriculum goals.

Visionary leadership

Standard 5 of the NBPTS refers to 'visionary leadership' as a framework of the modern library media center. It is the certified teacher-librarian who must have a vision of where the media center is going and share this vision with other school staff. The way in which the library media center specialist addresses changes in technology and teaching will heighten the level of achievement of the various learning communities within and outside the school.

The NBCT administrating the library will work toward integrating new technologies into the information literacy curriculum. The library media specialist is both technician and teacher. Entrusted with the job of purchasing and maintaining hardware and software, the media center administrator is also responsible for expanding connectivity with outside learning communities.

NBCT management duties

No longer is the library program director in the role of preserving and protecting the library collection at the expense of alienating teachers, students and administration of the school. The modern library media program manager has the chief goal of providing and expanding access to all learners. The modern library media program should be comfortable and welcoming. There are several ways to accomplish this.

- Encourage the formation of a library program advisory committee consisting of classroom teachers and school administrative staff. The library advisory committee should work together with the media specialist to establish goals based upon a vision of future information needs.
- Evaluating the progress of program development while maintaining a policy of open, inclusive, and expanded access to media center services.

Information Search Process

Carol Kuhlthau identified six stages of the Information Search Process.

- Initiation: The information seeker recognizes the need for information but is anxious and uncertain how to proceed.
- Selection: The quest for information considers topics based on personal interest, the requirements of the assignment, and the availability and location of information about the topic(s).
- Exploration: This is a stage typified by actions like locating information, reading, and digesting new information.
- Formulation: The researcher gains a focus. A clear perception of the topic(s) and the task becomes fixed in the learner's mind.

Copyright © Mometrix Media. You have been licensed one copy of this document for personal use only. Any other reproduction or redistribution is strictly prohibited. All rights reserved.

- Collection: The information obtained is material and pertinent to the research information objective. Information needs are specifically defined.
- Presentation: The information seeker moves to complete the research and develops a sense of satisfaction and possesses a confidence in understanding the various facets of the information topic.

Novels advance learning

Fiction has been a traditional and reliable way of creating an appreciation of literacy. A library media center's commitment to fiction titles is key to molding today's students into life long learners.
- Fiction opens up many avenues and possibilities.
- Children easily identify with the characters in selected fiction titles.
- Fiction titles can be found which fit the psychological, emotional, and learning styles of students of all ages and ability.
- Fiction titles can be focused on various academic subjects like Science and History. Reading of historical novels or other fiction titles can emphasize and reinforce learning acquired in other subject areas.
- Constant reading of fiction titles expands vocabulary skills and supports development of writing capabilities.

Advocacy key facts

Advocacy means the communication of ideas and to the community which supports learners. Advocacy has the following goals:
- Overarching Goals: Increasing visibility and awareness of the goals of the library media program is a key concern.
- Specific Goals: There may be specific targets for specialized advocacy. Perhaps there is need to win over the principal or the school board to what the library means toward student achievement and curriculum goals.
- Activities: This key component of advocacy means the wide array of concrete activities performed by media center staff in the interest of promoting facility use. It means reading programs, newsletters, literacy based contests. It can even mean personal contact or appearances by the library media specialist before groups which may support the library.
- Assessments: It is important for the media center manager to develop a system of advocacy measurement tools to gauge the effectiveness of the collection, its staff, and resources.

Laws of Library Science

In 1931, formulated a theory of books which is in use today. Ranganathan's Five Laws of Library Science are still accepted as the foundation of the modern library.
- Books are for use: This first law of library science is meant to free books and informational materials from any restraints and make information available to everyone.
- Every reader his book: While a reader may not like some books, it is axiomatic that everyone will be able to find a book they enjoy and profit from reading.

Copyright © Mometrix Media. You have been licensed one copy of this document for personal use only. Any other reproduction or redistribution is strictly prohibited. All rights reserved.

- Every book its reader: Specialized and seemingly unpopular material will eventually be sought by some reader.
- Save the time of the reader: The reader's enjoyment increases when it's easy to obtain the book which is being sought.
- The Library is a growing organism: Informational needs are always changing and the library must change and adapt to new conditions.

Literature for young people

Literature for young people is typically broken down into two components by the ALA.
- Literature for children is the category meant for children from birth to age fourteen.
- Literature for Young Adults is meant for youngsters from age ten to age eighteen.
- The categories are established by the ALA on the basis of its award system. There are several types of award given to writers of literature for these age groups and some of the awards may fall into both categories. This explains the overlap in age bracket which occurs from age ten to age fourteen.
- The ALA subdivisions which have established awards in literature for young people are the ALSC and the YALSA. ALSC is an acronym for Association for Library Service to children. YALSA means Young Adult Library Association.

Copyright © Mometrix Media. You have been licensed one copy of this document for personal use only. Any other reproduction or redistribution is strictly prohibited. All rights reserved.

ALSC and YALSA

Well-known awards in the field of children's literature are:
- YALSA means Young Adult Library Association. ALSC is an acronym for Association for Library Service to children. Both these ALA subdivisions have established awards in literature for young people.
- YALSA awards include: ALEX Award (adult books appealing to young readers); Best Books for Young Adults; Michael Printz Award.
- ALSC awards include: Caldecott Medal; Newbery Medal; Pura Belpre Medal; Coretta Scott King Award: Robert Sibert Medal.

Awards made by the ALA subdivisions are an easy way to find books that are thought to be excellent buying and reading choices for the library media center, but there are other guidelines, too. Literature for Today's Young Adults is an excellent and often used guideline for children's literature, as is Lukens Critical Handbook of Children's Literature.

Approaches to reading

Classroom reading strategies have evolved over the years and the various methods of teaching reading have become controversial issues. When conflicts affect the classroom, it can also be expected to affect the library media center. Most controversy centers upon the approaches to teaching of reading.

Reading was traditionally in the domain of the Language Arts teacher or the 'English teacher' as it was termed. The Language Arts or English teacher split time between grammar, writing, and literature studies. Literature studies included reading practice. Schools in many states have decreed that reading should be in a dedicated classroom with the reading teacher as the primary instructor. Reading specialists often focus on remedial reading and that very often begins in the early grades.

Electronic reading programs

Electronic reading programs are a source of controversy in many schools and libraries. Accelerated Reader is just one example of a popular electronic reading program. Students are directed and guided through the reading of a fiction or non-fiction book. The electronic reading program consists of a software formulation that measures comprehension levels of students. Electronic reading programs can monitor comprehension through the use of quizzes. The software also measures higher order thinking skills. Teachers and media specialists who use electronic reading programs appreciate the way the software evaluates for reading level and the ease with which it provides scores on quizzes. However, the method has its critics, too, and many educators feel that the method can discourage reading by removing the human element of it. Others criticize the electronic programs because they feel the electronic media focuses more on memorization than ability and appreciation of reading.

Copyright © Mometrix Media. You have been licensed one copy of this document for personal use only. Any other reproduction or redistribution is strictly prohibited. All rights reserved.

Interactive approach

The interactive approach is subjective but it can have positive rewards. The instructor makes a reading selection and monitors the reading. Afterward, the instructor use strategies of interacting with students to elucidate deeper meanings, and to shed light on problem areas. The interactive approach can be used either by the classroom teacher or the library media specialist providing literature instruction in one of the library classrooms. If the right literature has been selected, students will be most inclined to see themselves in various roles depicted in a literary work. Literature is a mirror of the human condition. Usually, students are very willing to reflect their own experiences in that mirror especially when the instructor asks the right questions. Interactive questions might be answered orally or in writing. Interactive questions might be: What would you have done in that character's place? What motivated that character? Could that have happened to you or to anyone you know?

Reinforcement and shaping

While educators are reluctant to admit of the extent of their use of behavioral teaching techniques, the methods developed by the behaviorists are used by educators on a daily basis.

- Reinforcement teaching is based on the assumption that desirable achievements and outcomes must be reinforced immediately. Early stages of learning require more frequent reinforcement but, as the student progresses, reinforcement should become more intermittent.
- Shaping is a technique which relies on the behavioral principles of reinforcement and repetitive training. Early on, the student would be given positive feedback even when the results are not exactly at the highest achievement level. However, the student is motivated by a desire for greater success and moves in the right direction as the instructor raises the standards.

Mastery learning

'Mastery learning' was a modification of the behaviorist theory of task analysis. Building upon task analysis, Bloom added one more layer. Material to be learned is still broken down into small units, just as it would be with the 'task analysis' model, but each small unit must be thoroughly digested before the learner moves on to succeeding units. Bloom's theories of mastery learning are the actual progenitors of later educational products like Accelerated Reader, an electronic reading program which does not allow the reader to progress to the next level until he/she has a thorough understanding of the previous level. Another form of mastery learning is integral to a method of learning theory called programmed instruction.

Copyright © Mometrix Media. You have been licensed one copy of this document for personal use only. Any other reproduction or redistribution is strictly prohibited. All rights reserved.

Supporting diverse abilities

Principle 7 of the Teaching Principles of School Library Media Programs is that the library media center must support diverse abilities, styles, and needs. One of the most objective places where one could find out how the diverse needs and abilities of America's student population are being met is the NAEP (National Assessment of Educational Progress).

The NAEP is often termed the 'government's report card' and measures educational performance statistics of various ethnic or gender groups. It provides annual statistics on SAT scores, state school rankings, and a variety of other data broken down and reported on the basis of age, gender, and ethnicity.

Library Power Initiative

The Library Power Initiative grew out of a 1988 forty million dollar initiative to reform, update and modernize school library media centers across the country. The funding organization was the DeWitt Wallace-Reader's Digest Fund. It is a model of investment in education which has been consistent with ALA program goals of turning school library programs into state-of-the art learning facilities. Its general purpose was to expand the reach of technologies into communities where infrastructure and resources were lacking. Inner-city schools with cash-strapped budgets were a favorite target of library improvement efforts. .

Library Power goals

Library Power was developed around six goals and has identified six core activities to effectuate these goals. Core activities are the following:

- Expand school library collections consistent with the subject matter taught.
- Flexible scheduling so that teachers, students, and other staff can take better advantage of library materials.
- Expanding and organizing the physical facility around access and services.
- Implementing collaborative planning and teaching into the larger school community.
- Training and staffing full-time library media specialists who will maintain connection with larger professional communities of library developers.
- Providing and funding ongoing professional development in university courses and professional organization like AASL, a subdivision of the American Library Association.

Library space organization

The following guidelines will help create an effective use of library physical space.

- Location of the school library should be a central location away from noisy and high traffic areas. Where possible, it is advantageous to have electronic access points to search technologies in outlying areas.
- The school library should have individual reading, listening, and viewing areas.
- Ideally, the school library media center should have areas set aside for small group activities and large group activities.
- Staff work areas should be established where the library media specialist can observe library traffic and activities while working on labeling, ordering, and other operational activities.
- The library media center should have a media production area where students and teachers can produce video, audio, and slides or other media.

Copyright © Mometrix Media. You have been licensed one copy of this document for personal use only. Any other reproduction or redistribution is strictly prohibited. All rights reserved.

- A conference room is desirable for planning and other activity, as is a computer access area.

Updating collections expenditures

- The LMS will be working toward the goals of keeping the collection up to date and matched to school curriculum. Each school year will be a time of evaluating what is in the collection and determining what materials need updating. There are certain questions the LMS must regularly consider:The copyright year of the library's most recent general knowledge encyclopedia? Consider electronic and print formats.The total holdings, additions, and expenditures of the library media center in the following areas: audio, video, book titles, and CD-ROMs. Note that these items should be broken down into three categories: number held, number acquired, and the dollar amount of the expenditure.
- How much did the library media center spend on subscriptions? This includes periodicals, online databases, newspapers and journals.

Effective collaborator

A school library media specialist must be an effective collaborator:
An effective collaborator in the library media center attends conferences, seminars and meetings in professional organizations and brings back useful and updated information.

- An effective LMS collaborator facilitates flexible scheduling by advocating for the removal of impediments. This involves diplomacy and tact as much as it involves urgency.
- An effective collaborator meets frequently with classroom teachers to plan structure and method of delivery of learning activities.
- An effective collaborator is a 'teacher of other teachers' and helps them to become independent and self-reliant users of information.
- An effective collaborator reaches out to other professional organizations to share insights and ideas, to aid research studies, and to advocate for modernization of media center development.

Computer versus information literacy

These terms are often used synonymously but they're not synonymous. The computer is a tool to obtain information; it requires knowledge of hardware and software functioning. Information literacy refers to being able to manipulate and use the material that is found in a variety of sources online and offline.
Computer literacy means knowing how to use a mouse, how to type, how to use software like word processing, database, spreadsheet, etc. More advanced computer literate users are adept at the mechanics of web search tools, Boolean operators, and are familiar with common hardware problems.
Information literacy involves knowing the importance and value of specific library resources like OPAC (online library catalog), periodical databases, and other electronic materials. It also involves extensive knowledge of traditional print materials and methods of cataloguing.

Library services web page

Any effective school library web page begins with a Home Page clearly identifying the location and name of the library. A home page is the first thing the user sees and should be simple, clear, and

Copyright © Mometrix Media. You have been licensed one copy of this document for personal use only. Any other reproduction or redistribution is strictly prohibited. All rights reserved.

direct in approach. Main categories of services should be represented on the home page in hyperlinks which can be followed when the user selects that information path. Graphics should be simple and not glitzy or distracting when they are used.

Categories with links which should be on the Home Page are the general library information detailing hours of operations and location of the facility, the online catalogue, a link to free online databases and subscription databases if the library has them, and any special conditions which may apply.

Using signs and posters

The use of signage in libraries has many positive advantages when used effectively.
- Libraries use signs, posters, and displays for many purposes: promotional activities, orientation, hygiene and safety, and to call attention to special areas.
- Signs are available at times when library staff may be busy dealing with patrons.
- Signs and posters are relatively inexpensive and do not overstrain the library budget.
- Signs and posters can be a welcoming positive force, particularly in areas where younger children are concerned. For other students and also for adult teachers, they serve to relieve anxiety.
- Signage should be consistent, clear, and simple. Rules and cautionary should be expressed in a positive manner rather than in a dictator-subject mode.

Orientation tours

School library media specialists frequently schedule an orientation tour with teachers, students, and school administrators.
- An orientation tour can help to encourage media center use and reveal the library as a friendly and supportive partner in information literacy.
- Tours are an effective way of reaching out to students and teachers. Orientation tours save time and increase efficiency in that many general issues can be addressed to an entire group rather than individually.
- Tours can be made more productive by adequate advance planning of stopping points on the tour and with handouts which can reinforce information when the groups return to classroom or offices.

Advocacy outreach campaigns

In times of shrinking library budgets, the school library media specialist must increase its efforts in advocacy. There are several ways in which the LMS can advocate as educators within their school districts.
- Write letters to the editor to newspapers, political representatives, and community social agencies calling attention to the ways in which school libraries contribute to academic achievement.
- Use the AASL Toolkit which provides standard letters which may be adapted for different audiences.
- Inform the public about the role of the library media specialist, particularly of their classification as instructors.
- Write letters to the NCES indicating your support for re-classification of library media support staff as instructors. This could result in the media center receiving a larger percentage of school funding.

Copyright © Mometrix Media. You have been licensed one copy of this document for personal use only. Any other reproduction or redistribution is strictly prohibited. All rights reserved.

Collaborating in professional communities

It is important that the library media specialist maintain and participate in professional organization like AASL. Collaboration with the larger community of learners makes each library media center a partner to improvement in the educational culture. The following activities are methods of participating outside professional communities.

- Participate in the 'Wiki" established online by the AASL for drafting new learning standards. This provides opportunity for the LMS to be a leader in advancing educational goals rather than a follower.
- Write a proposal explaining why you are the best candidate for a $3,000 grant awarded to a student learning how be a full-time media specialist in elementary or secondary schools.
- Take part in surveys and information gathering conducted by the AASL to contribute to understanding the state of school libraries across the nation. This is a way of participating in the two way flow of information between learning communities.

Bridges to all cultures

During the past decade, school districts and school library media center staff have become increasingly involved in other countries due to the influx of immigrants and to the global contact provided by modern technology. It is more important than ever that the media specialist teacher be knowledgeable about and continue learning about other cultures.

- Library Media Specialist Teachers may be partners in international library associations and conferences.
- Electronic communication techniques makes it possible to initiate cross-cultural assistance projects to train and assist school libraries of other countries.
- Under the supervision of the LMS, student may interact with international students in a way that befits and enlarges the understanding of history, customs, and beliefs.
- Library media specialists and teachers may undertake temporary positions abroad to enlarge upon their knowledge base and to share American values, customs and language with developing nations.

Improving Literacy program

This grant program focused on impoverished inner city schools was established as part of the No Child Left Behind initiative of the Bush administration. The program was evaluated in a 2005 study by the U.S. Department of Education and drew the following conclusions:

- Grantee schools were brought up to a level of equality with non-grantee schools and in some cases surpassed them without decreasing the amount of local money expended.
- Grantee schools used funds to update materials, extending hours of operation for the libraries, and expanded planning and collaboration time between classroom teachers and library instructors.
- The study showed an increase in library usage between the years 2003 and 2004.

Annual evaluations

The Library Media Specialist should outline a methodology to follow and pursue assessments goals in a step-by-step manner.

Copyright © Mometrix Media. You have been licensed one copy of this document for personal use only. Any other reproduction or redistribution is strictly prohibited. All rights reserved.

- Above all, the Library Media Specialist should be a leader. The first step in leadership is to organize a research effort.
- A second step might be to review literature, studies, and writings to see what others have done to meet literacy needs. The LMS can obtain information from larger professional communities and consult with professionals on media specialist online forums.
- Take a long look at the student and staff community of learners. What are the areas of interest? Who are the learners? What can be done to facilitate access to learning?
- Collect data using surveys, recording observations, and retrieving data from the electronic systems.
- Evaluate the validity of the research data.
- Weigh the data collected and set priorities.
- Implement the necessary changes.

Web 20

The World Wide Web began in the 1950s. Earlier versions were called Arpanet and known only to scientists and academics. The Web has undergone a revolution of change and innovation until now it is used by just about every household which has a computer. The term 'Web 2.0' is defined by the services the Web of today provides: Weblogs, linklogs, folksonomies, wikis, podcasts and web services which allow anyone to share information online. This sharing of information is not always accurate. It is of utmost importance for the library media specialist and classroom teacher to instruct students in the evaluation of information in terms of accuracy, timeliness, and convergence upon the subject being researched.

Podcasting

The word 'podcast' has meaning beyond the well-known I-pod, an audio device which allows the audience to listen to download and listen to music.
- 'Podcasting' currently includes video and a variety of voice recorded data which may be used for instructional purposes.
- One of the advantages of podcasting is that it engages students who are well-acquainted with its use. These students will benefit from producing their own podcasts or listening to podcast lectures provided free by prestigious universities which would be too expensive for many to attend.
- Another advantage is that the production software for producing podcasting is free and can be downloaded on the internet. Audacity is the name of one popular and free podcast software package used in production. It has versions created for both Mac and PC users.

Banned Books Week

Intellectual freedom is one of the ALA's Library Bill of Rights. The American Library Association believes in the ability of readers and library professionals to make positive intellectual decisions without censorship. Most attempts at censorship are intended to protect others, usually children, from certain types of information. Very often these attempts at protection override the freedom of speech which is guaranteed in the U.S. Constitution. The three chief topics for which books are challenged by organizations and individuals are: offensive language, sexual content, and unsuitability for certain age groups. The ALA has confidence that professional organizations and teachers have a responsibility to support intellectual freedom.

Copyright © Mometrix Media. You have been licensed one copy of this document for personal use only. Any other reproduction or redistribution is strictly prohibited. All rights reserved.

Challenged reading choices

The National Coalition Against Censorship assists educators when fiction books are challenged or when attempts are made to ban them. That organization provides support in the way of advocacy and publicity which favors intellectual freedom. The coalition files legal briefs in response to attempts to thwart 1st Amendment Rights. It advises teachers and librarian media specialists how to file complaints about free speech rights and provides forms which inform librarians and teachers about the data that is needed for a successful challenge.

The American Library Association also provides support and advice to educators when challenges are issued. They sponsor the Intellectual Freedom Action Network to monitor challenges and provide legal support to academic communities which foster free speech.

Special education students

The library media center can help to meet the needs of special education students in the following areas:
- Computer assisted instruction can empower special needs students to work independently and productively.
- The school library media center is a resource to students, teachers, and families to learn about the special needs learning environment.
- The school library media center is a place where the library media specialist can meet with and collaborate in the formulation of strategies to meet the needs of students with disabilities.
- The school library media center is a place where concrete strategies of development, equipment, and methods of operation can be directed toward students with mild to moderate learning and behavioral problems.
- The school library media center can provide access to all library resources by the creation of a physical spatial and technological environment which is geared toward students with special needs.

The technology room in the library media center affords an opportunity for socialization that the 'real world' may not provide to students with disabilities or learning impairment.
- Consider the student who uses a teen chat program to develop positive peer interaction through email and live online discourse.
- The student who needs a wheelchair would benefit from the information resources in a media center which has been remodeled with accessible space for wide aisles, wheelchair height computer terminals, and materials stored on shelves that student can reach without asking for the assistance of library staff.
- The library media center can be a supportive model for visually impaired students who may be assisted by Braille software programs or adaptive keyboards.

IEP team

The library media specialist is an important part of the Individual Improvement Plan (IEP) team:
- The LMS can participate in team meetings by acting as a consultant with regard to basic strategies aimed at specific and individual problems.

Copyright © Mometrix Media. You have been licensed one copy of this document for personal use only. Any other reproduction or redistribution is strictly prohibited. All rights reserved.

- The library media specialist can provide valuable resource information on a variety of special needs definitions by compiling a list of print, media, and online information sources on a particular physical or emotional limitation.
- The library media specialist may act as a co-teacher in the objectives established by the IEP process. Co-teaching can underscore and target the learning goals of the special needs student. The media specialist's role has evolved from one that facilitates to one which provides direct instruction.
- The library media specialist is an expert in the array of technologies available and useful in the acquisition of learning and information skills of special needs students.

National legislative initiatives

Legislation mandating broader access for special needs individuals have been on the books for many decades. However, three legislative initiatives are of particular note for library media specialists:
- The Americans with Disabilities Act of 1990 requires that reasonable accommodation be made to individuals with a 'disability'. It mandates that public facility access be expanded and broadened so that all persons can benefit from public services and public accommodations.
- The Assistive Technology Act of 1998 provides an avenue of funding for school educational programs which extend access to students (and others) with special needs in the schools and workplace. As the result of this program, states receive more federal aid which can be passed down to the schools which provide assistive technologies to learning.
- The Disabilities Education Improvement Act of 2004 provides for universal design of physical and technological components of learning.

Co-teaching structures

Marilyn Friend's rendering of co-teaching strategies may have different structures:
- Two partners in a teaching collaboration share the classroom. One of the instructors leads the classroom activities while the other observes, assesses areas which need development, and maintains data.
- Parallel teaching involves two instructors who are active at the same time in a divided classroom area. The two groups may receive different alternating instruction or simultaneous instruction.
- Station teaching can involve two or more instructors who are located in different areas of the classroom. Classroom instruction is broken down into component parts which are learned at the various stations.
- Alternative teaching is a common method of collaboration and may take place in the same classroom or in altogether different areas. Two instructors take turns covering course material.

IDEIA

The Disabilities Education Improvement Act of 2004 (IDEIA) is one of the most recent legislative initiatives aimed a broadening the scope of access to disabled and special needs learners. It defines

Copyright © Mometrix Media. You have been licensed one copy of this document for personal use only. Any other reproduction or redistribution is strictly prohibited. All rights reserved.

design standards for building construction and the location of facilities and technology within the buildings.   The Act has the purpose of making school buildings and library media centers accommodating to learners with special needs at the same time for all students. By incorporating universal design into buildings, the added costs of remodeling of existing buildings may be reduced or allayed altogether. The principles of universal design are directed toward better access to information technology, telecommunications, transportation to and from schools. This places less stress on the ongoing budgetary concerns of the library media specialist.

Accommodative techniques

Two groups of students which may benefit from the library media specialist's expertise in accommodating all students are:
- Students who have difficulty in following instructions and working independently.   The library media specialist-teacher can accommodate this type of students by posting rules and activity schedules and using cue cards and reminders posted around the media center.   Such students may also benefit from CAI (Computer Assisted Instruction) since the computer 'remembers' and constantly poses the question or task.
- Hearing impaired students may benefit from accommodations which include better lighting so that they can read cue cards and reminders. Instructions for media center activities might be better understood and acted upon if they are given in print rather than orally.   Similarly, the wide use of available assistive hearing technologies like Braille translators would be a positive step in accommodating hearing impaired students.

Presentations to visually impaired

Six recommendations made by the ALA's Library Technology department for presenting materials to visually impaired students are:
- Use high-contrast text. Replace toner when necessary so that printing characteristics stand out.
- Avoid decorative fonts. Stick with plain and simple text of a font size between 14 to 18 points. Arial and Tahoma are two fonts the ALA recommended in its report.
- Use bold type and avoid italics or printing the material entirely in upper case.
- When different colored lettering is required for banners or posters, use only dark-blue or greens.   Too many print colors will make text difficult to read for people with poor vision.
- Avoid glossy, magazine style paper.   The glare emanating from these can be distracting to persons with poor vision.
- Writing text in short sentences with adequate line spacing will make reading easier for the visually impaired.

Guidelines for new LMS

A newly appointment library media specialist must:
- Learn the Process. Examine recent budgets to determine the accounting methods and categories used in previous budgets. Identify funding sources. Consider sources of 'windfall' funding, i.e., funding from gifts, fines, grants, and other non-regular sources.
- Involve key people. Key people include the principal and any other school officials who have authority over expenditures.
- Be prepared to justify all expenditures when offering your budget for approval. Show how expenditures you wish to make for the library media center program will positively

Copyright © Mometrix Media. You have been licensed one copy of this document for personal use only. Any other reproduction or redistribution is strictly prohibited. All rights reserved.

affect student achievement. Demonstrate how your budget supports the school district's curriculum and objectives.

- The library media specialist must be able to respond quickly to urgent budgetary needs and differentiate between those which can be accomplished later. The library budget you submit should have clear priorities. It is a rare occasion when all budget request items are granted.

Extending center services

It is the responsibility of the library media specialist to provide access to and make available the necessary resources to achieve curriculum goals. The LMS does this through the development of a systematic, organized collection of library media materials.

- Access for students can be facilitated by such things as providing a 'new books' shelf or display to alert students when new materials arrive. Posting clear and appropriate signage is another way of guiding students to information resources.
- Access for teachers can be facilitated by the maintenance of an online cataloguing system and links to professional communities and organizations like AECT, AASL, and ALA. Online subscription services to research and reference databases do a great deal to facilitate professional growth and learning.

Literature selection effectiveness

The school library media specialist must keep abreast of current literature by reading journals which specialize in the review of children's and young adult literature.

- Publisher's lists, content reviewers, and participation in professional organizations will keep the library media center specialist up-to-date and moving forward in collection development.
- The library media specialist must be aware of new literature titles and the controversies they may create. By the same token, the library media specialist should have knowledge of classic and traditional titles which have stirred controversy. The media specialist must collaborate with the classroom teacher to become articulate resources for school administrators to employ in the cause of intellectual freedom.
- The library media specialist should circulate informational literature materials to teachers on topics that impact curriculum.

Broadening information accessibility

It is important for the library media specialist to develop flexible circulation loan policies which encourage information literacy and provide equal access to all users.

- Borrowing policies must be clearly set forth and followed. Information about library policies should extend outside the media center to parents and the larger community.
- The library media specialist should be aware of the need to provide library services to home-schooled children and young adults. Online computer links with password access should be established for the benefit of the student.
- There are times when, through collaboration with classroom teachers or other staff, the library media specialist should provide book carts to the classroom with advance selected materials.

Education technology procedures

Copyright © Mometrix Media. You have been licensed one copy of this document for personal use only. Any other reproduction or redistribution is strictly prohibited. All rights reserved.

The duties of the school library media specialist with regard to technology are:

- The library media center must establish an accurate and efficient information retrieval system.
- The retrieval system should be easy to operate and navigation should be logical, apparent, easy to read and understand.
- The school library media center can extend to outside terminals by the establishment of electronic access to databases and links to other library reference resources.
- The library media center can provide search and technical assistance when students or teacher encounter 'blocks' or other impediments to research. Intervention and assistance is needed when administrative filters block legitimate search mechanics.
- The library media specialist should maintain confidentiality in the use of student assessment records and information retrieval. Passwords should be set and privacy policies strictly observed by all staff members.

Duties with students and teachers

The library media specialist works with students and teachers in the following ways:

- The library media specialist and other media center staff must assist all users in identifying and locating information, and provide assistance in the use of technology.
- The school media center staff can collaborate with classroom teachers during library class time to pre-select materials for specific curriculum assignments. Materials can be posited at 'stations' around the library in order to assist in 'crowd control'.
- The school library media center can set up areas for small group discussion and collaborative work.
- The school media center staff can directly assist and train students in the use of assistive technologies for the hearing or visually impaired, or guide those with other physical disabilities to accessible areas.

Management actions

The management actions of the school library media specialist support curriculum goals:

- As the media center manager, the forward thinking library media specialist assumes responsibility for training and orientation of adult and volunteer staff in a variety of ways.
- The LMS teaches after-school courses for teachers and instructional aides in the use of educational technology and information retrieval systems. Teacher orientation is as necessary to teachers as it is for students. The library media specialist must make clear the distinction between the various types of online database and reference systems.
- As a management activist, the library media specialist might wish to participate in committees, seminars, and professional development activities in the interest of being a lifelong learner and an advocate for information literacy.

Home page headings

A logical and standardized library media center homepage can be a welcome pathway to information literacy. There is no single method which would fit every need or subscription. However, there are general concerns which, if adhered to, will make information retrieval a desirable rather than a frustrating process.

Copyright © Mometrix Media. You have been licensed one copy of this document for personal use only. Any other reproduction or redistribution is strictly prohibited. All rights reserved.

- A homepage design should be kept simple and uncluttered. Basic graphic elements can enhance the experience. Be careful in construction to avoid a distracting design.
- The homepage should have clear links to key elements: Online catalogue of library resources, associated libraries, library policies, community links, and a series of links to online research subscription services. Visual space is the only limit to the number of links, but keep the audience in mind. Students and even teachers can be overwhelmed by an overwhelming number of information choices which greet them when they log on to a library information system.

Online information databases

When constructing links to online subscription services, it is best to aim group categories of information toward the intended audience. The library media specialist might look at other library home pages to obtain ideas on logical design. Then it is a matter of arranging categories and sub-categories. The following categories might link to 'second' pages in the web navigation system: Health and Science categories; Professional development and scholarly research categories; Student and children's resources. Depending on the number of subscriptions, it might be feasible to establish a separate page for student online subscription services which provide access to interactive learning.

Web page design criteria

There are standards questions a student or teacher may use to evaluate web page design:
- Is the page designed for easy navigability? Are the links clearly labeled and visible? Is there a way to return to the previous page? Are the links active? Does the site contain 'dead' links which are in need of updating?
- Does the site allow interactive usage? Is there a place for the visitor to contact the Web site administrator?
- Is the page format appropriate? Does the page content contain more than the eye can see? Is the font size appropriate or too small?
- Consider graphic design aesthetics? Is there too much color? Too little contrast? Is vital information pushed to the side or put in areas where it is not easily seen?

Listserv

A 'listserv' is a type of electronic forum wherein users can address large groups of people with similar interests and rich experience. It is a method of collaboration which is useful to library media specialists and to school library media center patrons.
A 'listserv' usually contains a variety of topics. It is considered rude and careless to post comments or ask questions in the wrong areas. It is important to know beforehand if the desired information is one of the topics of that listserv.
It is possible to join or 'subscribe' to more than one professional group at a time and listservs offer the opportunity to 'subscribe' or 'unsubscribe', depending on whether they meet the user's information needs.

Websites improving self-expression

Three websites aimed at improving student literacy and self-expression are:

Copyright © Mometrix Media. You have been licensed one copy of this document for personal use only. Any other reproduction or redistribution is strictly prohibited. All rights reserved.

- The Diary Project at http://www.diaryproject.com/ invites students to post written observations, notes, or commentary about their lives. It was inspired by the popular and well-known young adult title Zlata's Diary.
- Kidscribe (at http://www.kidscribe.org/) advertises itself as a 'bilingual site for kid authors'. It offers the opportunity for cross-learning between cultures. Postings upon that site are in English and Spanish and it appears to serve a wide range of ages.
- The National Film Board of Canada sponsors a web site aimed at young writers in early elementary school age groups. It provides colorful games, animations and interactive pre-programmed possibilities for self-expression in writing and the graphic arts.   Its website address is: http://www.nfbkids.ca.

Paraphrasing versus plagiarism

The standards of professional ethics for the school library media specialist establishes clear guidelines for avoiding and discouraging plagiarism. Very often a person believes they are paraphrasing (a legitimate use of copyrighted material) when they are, in fact, plagiarizing. Some students believe that, by rearranging the structure of a sentence, they are avoiding plagiarism. Others may feel they are paraphrasing when they substitute synonyms for words used in copyrighted material, but they also may be plagiarizing.
Avoiding plagiarism when paraphrasing means that the writer thoroughly understands the concepts explained in copyrighted material, and then writes a translation of their meaning in original language. If a small phrase must be borrowed from the original, it should be clearly marked by the use of quotation marks and credit should be given to the author.

Flexible access

There are differences in the ways schools operate their schedules and it is inevitable that schedules will conflict with library operations.   Many school schedules are 'fixed', that is, they consist of a set number of classes and a specific period of teacher preparation time. The purpose of set schedules is so that the central office administrators can know where and when teachers are located, what they are doing, and how they may be contacted.   The inflexibility of such schedules doesn't utilize library programs to best advantage.   Flexible scheduling allows the media specialist to bring classes to the media center according to a media center schedule planned around information literacy.   The NBPTS recognizes flexible scheduling as a 'best teaching practice'.

Ethical use procedures

Paraphrasing can be a valuable adjunct and aid to learning.   However, there are procedures one can follow to avoid it, particularly for students who have limited background in written communication. The library or classroom media specialist might set the following rules:
- Read and reread the original copyrighted material until it is thoroughly digested and understood. Then put the material aside.
- Jot down some ideas your own words regarding how you intend to use the material.   Use note cards to annotate key concepts or ideas.   Then write a paragraph in your own words to express key concepts.
- A final step is to integrate the sentences into an entire paragraph expressing the ideas gained from reading.   If direct quotations must be used, they are to be used sparingly.

Copyright © Mometrix Media. You have been licensed one copy of this document for personal use only.
Any other reproduction or redistribution is strictly prohibited. All rights reserved.

Literature appreciation

ALA Standard 5 of information literacy is aimed at developing a program of literature appreciation and other forms of creative expression in the library media center. Elementary grade literature programs are commonly conducted in or reinforced by active media center reading programs. The library media specialist at ABC School District has assigned a book called 'My Brother Sam is Dead'.

The LMS stops reading at critical points and asks students who are formed in groups to jot down words and ideas obtained from the reading selection. Each group gets a chance to narrow down the topics and ideas chosen to one which are most relevant to the reading text.

At chapter intermissions, each group will be directed to use encyclopedia online and offline sources to write a brief paragraph on the topic the group has chosen.

Language Arts writing programs

Classroom teachers commonly rely on a 5-step process to develop writing skills of their students. The steps are a variation of the following: pre-writing, drafting, editing, revision, and publishing.

One of the learning and teaching principles of school library media programs emphasizes support for curriculum development and collaboration with classroom teachers. Accordingly, the library media specialist may develop strategies which support writing goals:

- Learn the specific methods being used by the Language Arts classroom teacher. There are many different approaches employed by users of the five step writing scenario.
- Put up media center posters outlining the five steps of the writing process.
- Organize a study group to assist in research of topics integral to the writing assignment project.

Copyright © Mometrix Media. You have been licensed one copy of this document for personal use only. Any other reproduction or redistribution is strictly prohibited. All rights reserved.

Information literacy and kingergarten

The library media specialist can aid kindergarten students in making the connection between the outside world and media center books. Very often the classroom teacher will introduce students to common signs by a walk on the sidewalk or playground outside the school. Students are urged to note signage which they see and are then asked to recollect the signs when back in the classroom. The librarian-teacher might do the following:

- Make connections between books and the real world by reading from one of the many fiction books dealing with this topic. A book by author Nancy Parent might be a good choice. A sample title: The Stop Sign.
- A final 'project' might be done in the media center to reinforce the learning connection. The students could draw a road of their own with simple road signs along the way. It is important that the connection between real world, media center, and learning be made over a long period of time.

Multicultural theme elements

The quality of materials is always important and that concern is crucial to the selection of multicultural non-fiction and fiction. The library media specialist should consider the following:

- The authority and background knowledge of the author can be a useful guide in selection of appropriate literature. Awards from library professional organizations provide a facile guide for media specialists with limited time.
- Respect for the content and for the persons depicted. Stereotypes of speech, manner, or dress are inappropriate. A condescending tone is harmful to the reading audience.

Multiculturalism

The school library media specialist should exhibit leadership in the following areas:

- The LMS and other staff must comport themselves in a way that respects and appreciates student diversity.
- The media specialist can support bilingual and multicultural student groups in the media center. Activities may include book discussion and the invitation of notable outside speakers to student instruction in the library media center.
- The library media specialist can develop and multicultural themes by the use of graphic design elements, posters, statues, artwork, and photos which depict smaller communities of learners as part of a larger community.
- The media specialist teacher can guide students in group discussion of cultural issues.

Cyber bullying

Several recent studies have determined that the expansion of information technology has created a new twist to student bullying. Standard 8 of the Information Literacy Standards for Student Learning prohibits this unethical use of technology, yet studies have shown that a large number of students have been subjected online to hurtful or threatening messages which uses email, IM messaging, cell phone text messaging, personal websites, and other technologies. The library media specialist can do the following:

Develop media center and school policies regarding appropriate use and actions which might follow when ethical standards are not observed.

Copyright © Mometrix Media. You have been licensed one copy of this document for personal use only. Any other reproduction or redistribution is strictly prohibited. All rights reserved.

Inform parents and students that all attempts at cyber bullying will be taken seriously and explored. Parents and students should also be informed of possible legal or criminal investigation of such concerns.

Reflective practice strategies

The library media specialist should implement an action plan to increase efficiency of operations. An action plan embodies a self-assessment combined with meaningful collaboration:

- Develop a research procedure and agenda. Develop toolkits to assist teachers in assessing student progress in informational development. Distribute data about the successful relationship between successful library media centers and student achievement.
- Examine past practices for the most successful kind of collaboration efforts which have achieved curriculum goals. Learn how to overcome resistance to collaboration which stems from overworked schedules or lack of focus on curriculum objectives.
- Compile evidence and research data to support the goals of the media center particularly as it relates to student achievement. Use the data to increase support and collaboration from other school staff.

Advocacy toolkits

It's important to funding and support that school staff and the general public realize the contribution the school media center makes to student success. Here are some steps the library media specialist can take:

- Be sure your school's homepage has an accessible link to the library media center web page. Be sure that the media center page has your name and contact telephone number and encourage people to contact you for information.
- Include a profile of yourself and your staff. Describe personal achievements, goals, interests, and hobbies. This aids in accessibility to resources at the same time that it avoids bureaucratic stereotypes.
- Use real photos on your website, not overused clip art. Write an article regularly in the school newspaper or school calendar or other publications sent to community residents.

Software assessment tools

Several software assessment tools are available to the school library media specialist:

- Student technical literacy can be measured with a product called TechLiteracy Assessment sold by the learning.com company. It's a graduated program which uses interactive response to find areas where the student requires further development.
- There are a wide array of software aimed at the teaching and assessment of reading skill. The Wireless Generation is just one. mCLASS Reading is an assessment reading program which features connectivity to thousands of book from leading educational publishers, hundreds of which are published in Spanish Language versions.
- Pearson is an educational publisher which can compare student performance against the benchmarks set by individual state standards. It sells several software products to measure student literacy.

Middle school information literacy

Copyright © Mometrix Media. You have been licensed one copy of this document for personal use only. Any other reproduction or redistribution is strictly prohibited. All rights reserved.

Planning a session for information literacy is key to a successful outcome. There are several factors to consider during the planning stage:

- Audience: The media specialist should consult with the classroom teacher to determine general achievement levels of four classes of eighth grade middle-school students. The number of students in a single class is always something to consider as it impacts other areas of facility and materials planning.
- Purpose: A specific purpose should be set for each session. Limit the classes to one concrete objective. An example of a concrete objective would be to 'Evaluate the Quality of Web Pages'.
- Time constraints: Allow thirty minutes learning time for each class. The classroom teacher will determine the week(s) in which literacy instruction will take place.
- Facilities: A computer lab in the library would be ideal, but not always possible. Workstations should be equipped with a Web browser, word processor, and networked to at least one printer.

Site map

A 'site map' is a general outline of a web site. A look at a well-constructed 'site map' will allow the user to see how the various links are connected to the 'top' headings on the Homepage. As each website may have a different construction, a site map is a way of learning the most efficient way of tracking through the site to obtain the desired information.
The library media specialist who constructs a site for their school media center must update the site when necessary. Pages will be deleted or added, and new links may be established. It is important to remember to update the site map at the same time. Another consideration for the library media specialist is to avoid jargon and language acronyms which might confuse the user. Accessibility to information is important to student learners and the media specialist can facilitate access by logical and clear design.

Fair use controversy

Standard 8 of the information literacy standards proscribes 'ethical behavior in regard to information and information technology'. While the laws regarding 'fair use' are most clearly established with regard to print material, there has been considerable controversy in the interpretation of the copyright laws with regard to information technology. The EFF (Electronic Frontier Foundation) founders believe that anything put up on the Internet should be free to everyone. The ALA and affiliated organizations believe that existing copyright laws for print materials should be strictly applied to the Web and to the Internet. The basic four rules of copyright should be well known by media specialist teachers:
Is the use educational or commercial? Aside from that first concern, the other three rules apply to type of information, the amount of information being used, and whether the author of the information will lose income as the result of its use by others.

Preparing hardware technology

Standard 1 of the information literacy standards proscribes efficient and effective access to information. Teaching information literacy to school students requires expertise in technology management.

Copyright © Mometrix Media. You have been licensed one copy of this document for personal use only. Any other reproduction or redistribution is strictly prohibited. All rights reserved.

Before the information literacy class begins, the information literacy teacher should make sure that hardware and software is ready for use.

- Turn on all the PC terminals to see if they are all properly functioning and loaded with standard software. If applicable to the lesson plan, be sure that the software allows connection to the internet. Are all terminals using the same software versions and is the filtering software up to date?
- Some schools have dedicated technology assistants to assist in problems which are beyond the scope of the information literacy teacher. Be sure such personnel are available and notified of information literacy class schedules.

Distance learning

Standard Five of the National Board for Professional Teaching Standards mentions 'leading innovation through the library media program'. Distance learning does just that when the library media specialist develops access for students who are disabled, impaired, or isolated from the school for any reason. There are various ways of extending educational opportunities to those outside the classroom and the methods used are ever expanding, as is the population served.

Distance learning has gone through several generations, the first of which were known as 'correspondence courses'. The current generation of web-based distance learning may have the following component technologies to deliver instruction: Broadcast, CD-Rom, video conferencing, and Podcast. Podcasting is becoming increasingly popular as prestige schools like Stanford and others put classroom lectures into the format and distribute them freely. Internet education can deliver content either synchronously or asynchronously.

No Child Left Behind Act

Standard Five of the National Board for Professional Teaching Standards mentions 'leading innovation through the library media program'. Innovation in leadership means collaboration with parents in distance learning. Library media specialist teachers are urged to implement school district action plans recommended by the NCLB legislation:

- Meet often to collaborate with district parents in the actual writing of parent involvement policies.
- Include parents in program improvement plans.
- Distribute an annual report card on the performance of schools inclusive of distance learning objectives.
- Inform parents if a school is low performing, provide transfer options for low performing schools, and provide free tutoring for underachieving students.

Distance learning teacher evaluation

The distance education teacher must meet the same state standards as the certified classroom teacher:

- The teacher must have credentials in the field in which he/she is teaching.
- Additional expertise in technology is required. Online teachers must provide regular feedback and communicate clear objectives. Assessment response should be prompt and accurate. It is helpful if the teacher has experienced online learning as a student.
- The teacher should have a comprehensive understanding and familiarity with the student's special needs environment.

Copyright © Mometrix Media. You have been licensed one copy of this document for personal use only. Any other reproduction or redistribution is strictly prohibited. All rights reserved.

- The teacher is competent in the use of data obtained through assessment technology and reformulates teaching strategies to fit the student's weaknesses and in a way that reinforces strengths.
- The teacher initiates projects and assignments for the student and monitors them to conclusion. Learning goals must clearly set forth and maintained at appropriate state and national levels. Assessment should be efficient and objective in determining whether the student meets curriculum goals.

Attention Deficit Disorder

Standard Two of the National Board for Professional Teaching Standards refers to the essential skill called 'Knowledge of Teaching and Learning'. The concept extends to students afflicted with this problem which can delay or derail learning. The library media specialist, as well as the classroom teacher, must adapt. The following methods may be of assistance with the ADD student:
- Read books and share information which provide a better understanding of the conditions. Focus on the topic and not the individual student in order to protect rights of privacy and confidentiality.
- Make observation of the student to learn when the unusual behavior is most likely to occur. Sometimes the environment can be arranged to ameliorate situations which aggravate the condition.
- Collaborate with parents and obtain further insight and input into disruptive behaviors. Similarly, the media specialist can collaborate with the school counselor or classroom aide to develop strategies.

Traditional versus information literacy

Traditional literacy and information literacy are intertwined. A foundation of traditional literacy is the most important pathway to understanding informational literacy. Though traditional grammar, spelling, and literary structure may seem to have fishtailed off the road on the Information Highway, the student without a firm basis in traditional literacy will start the race for success behind his better-read counterparts.

The library media specialist and classroom teacher must encourage the reading of fiction and non-fiction print materials. The classroom and the media center should be made accommodating, attractive, and friendly and the collection should reflect a wide range of interests.

Emphasize the importance of reading books to parents at every opportunity. Encourage students to use their own personal interests as a pathway to future literacy skills.

Literary coach criteria

The hiring of a library media specialist teacher as a literacy coach meets at least two criteria of the National Board for Professional Teaching Standards. Aside from benefiting from the specialized knowledge in teaching and learning, the literacy coach also indicates that the school district is aimed at meeting Standard Five: Leading Innovation through the Library Media Program.
- The literacy coach can put together a collaborative team and manage it with the same degree of fervor reserved for the management of the football team. The literacy coach coordinates the efforts of administrators, content and remedial teachers, and ESL teachers when applicable.

Copyright © Mometrix Media. You have been licensed one copy of this document for personal use only. Any other reproduction or redistribution is strictly prohibited. All rights reserved.

- The literacy coach conducts a school wide literary assessment which includes information and technology literacy.
- The literacy coach provides a forum wherein team members can relate problems they encounter in their specific environments so that all can work together toward resolution and higher achievements.

Evaluating web sites

Accuracy, Authority, Currency, Objectivity and Coverage are the five basic criteria used to judge the validity of web site information.

- Accuracy: Know which websites are likely to employ fact checkers and responsible editors.
- Authority: Know whether the publisher of the site is a known and reputable organization. It is easy to construct a website which gives the appearance of authority yet provides no information regarding the publisher's credentials or expertise.
- Objectivity: Know the purpose of the web site. Does it try to inform by revealing all sides of an issue or does it promote a single viewpoint? Is the web site self-promoting?
- Currency: Is the information current? Does the site refer to outdated studies? Does the site provide enough information so that you could trace it back to its source yourself? Using old information is a favorite trick of people trying to persuade you to adopt a particular viewpoint.
- Coverage: Is the coverage sparse? Does the site tell the whole story? Space limitations on web pages often result in abbreviated information.

Web page categories

One may choose different categories of grouping for web pages but most people would concur with the following types: Entertainment, Business and Marketing, Reference and Information, News, Advocacy, and Personal Pages.

Keep in mind that some web sites may combine these general categories. It is therefore all the more important to be able to recognize the characteristics which define their basic purpose and functions.

The popular site MySpace may contain useful information but its chief purpose is to provide entertainment. So it is with sports pages. This does not mean that the information contained on an entertainment site cannot be used for other study purposes, however. One may obtain useful information such as health related research as to the frequency of sports injuries and their impact. At the same time, newspapers try to provide objective information but a great deal of their content aims at entertainment.

Recognition of the various types of web pages is important and saves time for the business seeker:

- Business Pages: A very strict example of business pages are those presented on the website investopedia.com. That site provides information on finance, investing, and many other commercial operations in the U.S. and around the world.
- Entertainment Pages: HBO or MySpace have web pages devoted to their chief concern which is attracting people to their site through entertainment products.
- Reference Pages: These can be reliable subscription sites like the Encyclopedia Brittanica or Encarta. Using a 'portal' like a school library gateway provides access to many sites of this type.

Copyright © Mometrix Media. You have been licensed one copy of this document for personal use only. Any other reproduction or redistribution is strictly prohibited. All rights reserved.

- Advocacy: The American Library Association site advocates for library systems around the world.
- News: Most newspapers have corresponding web sites usually identified by the name of the newspaper followed by a dot com.
- Personal Pages: These are set up by individuals for their own individual purposes.

Questions for research paper

Standards 1, 2, and 3 of the nine information literacy standards require that the student access and use information effectively.   The student must begin by asking several types of essential questions which define the task:
- Purpose: What is the point of the task?   What is the evidence for thinking one way or the other?
- Subsidiary Questions: Clarify the research task by asking how to best define the topic. What are the different meanings and implications of the topic? Where will the information lead in the end?   Is my present knowledge reliable and complete?   Where can I look to add to the body of knowledge required by the research task?
- Organizing questions: What strategy will I use to get information? How will I plan the strategy I use?

Elementary versus secondary school

The nine standards of information literacy apply equally to secondary and elementary school students. The first three of the nine standards are geared toward the use of information; the second three are aimed at independent learning and research skills; the third three standards of information literacy are guidelines for the responsible use and access to information.
However, the levels of functioning are applied a different levels in the elementary grades. The type and depth of material being used is a key difference.   Standard 1 of information literacy for Grades K-2, for example, requires students to tell how they know something is true or false regarding a Life Skills class. The application of Standard 1 of information literacy to grades 9-12 of a Health class requires students to be familiar with a variety of governmental and private organizations which provide information to the consumer.

NBCT status advantages

The state of North Carolina leads the list of top ten states in terms of the number of successful NBCT candidates.   The advantages extended to teachers and media specialists having this certification are indicative of the recognition given this accreditation.
- Candidates in North Carolina have their $2300 entrance fee to the program paid by the state, in addition to extra hours granted to work on portfolio. Other states have adopted some variation on this model.
- Some states have increased salary scales to accommodate the NBCT level of achievement.
- NBCT candidates have the support of professional organizations and mentor networks to assist them through the process of certification.
- While National Board Certification is an area of debate in some circles, there are research studies which support the view that higher professional standards attained by this certification have resulted in higher student achievement standards.

Obtaining certification

Copyright © Mometrix Media. You have been licensed one copy of this document for personal use only. Any other reproduction or redistribution is strictly prohibited. All rights reserved.

The National Board Certification for Professional Teaching Standards designates two important categories critical to certification objectives. Candidates must consider both categories when making a choice regarding which certification to seek.

- Age categories are in four groups, designated as follows: EC or Early Childhood (ages 3-8); MC or Middle Childhood (ages 7-12); EA or Early Adolescence (ages 11-15) ; AYA or Adolescence and Young Adulthood (ages 14-18). Note that the age brackets are intended to be overlapping.
- The second important category of certification is in the subject area. The categories established by the Board Certification process acknowledge the learning capacities of different age groups, and the practical concerns of the library media specialist being required to teach 'across the board' to all ages.

ECYA certification

The ECYA certification in Library Media extends from ages 3-18 and encompasses a variety of skills. Standard One of the NBPTS recommendations refers to Knowledge of Learners in the broadest sense. The skills requirements to meet this standard are:

The certified library media specialist must have knowledge of basic human growth and development. This includes an awareness of various learning styles, and the differences in learning capacities between age group categories. The certified library media specialist is aware of the cognitive differences between child, adolescent, and adult learners.

The certified library media specialist is able to use the fundamental skills and knowledge and apply it to students of all ages and abilities. The NBCT must be able to demonstrate how this knowledge can be effectively applied in diverse settings and student populations.

Principles of program administration

A school library media program should move toward the improvement of learning through support of educational and curriculum goals.

- Licensing and certification of at least one full-time media specialist is in the interest of student achievement and effective information literacy programs.
- The successful library media program should be relevant to the size of the student population. It should meet the needs of other teachers, school administration and support staff.
- The school library media program should always seek support from school administration and authorities.
- The establishment of long-range plans consistent with the educational curriculum should be fundamental to the school library media center.
- Assessment: A successful school library media program requires constant assessment of its capabilities and reach. Assessment should not be an insular process; the library media specialist should reach out to others in a collaborative effort to recognize areas of strength or weakness in the program.
- Collaboration: It is of vital concern to collaborate with administrators and school board members to insure sufficient funding to meet the needs of the student population with regard to educational goals.
- Staff Development: Staff development and ongoing professional training is important in keeping up to date with the academic community's informational needs.
- Concrete Objectives: Goals and objectives of the library media program should be concrete and determinate. The library media specialist should be well versed and ready to explain them and to support them with facts and figures.

Copyright © Mometrix Media. You have been licensed one copy of this document for personal use only.
Any other reproduction or redistribution is strictly prohibited. All rights reserved.

- **Effective Management:** Effective management of the physical facility and support staff is an important and vital component in achieving curriculum goals of the library media program.

Principle 2 objectives

Principle 2 of Program Administration refers to the necessity of having a licensed library media specialist in the school library to direct and management the media center. Administrative activities under Principle 2 include the following:
- Interaction with personnel beyond the school media center. Attend and participate in school board activities and professional seminars.
- Maintain currency of library holdings and elevate professional standards in teaching, learning, information access, and supervision of staff.
- Collaborate with teachers and outside professionals to gain support and feedback for the program.
- Be engaged in performance appraisals of other staff. Provide constructive guidance for further professional development.
- Maintain connection with outside professional organizations like the AASL, and AECT. Stay current with new developments. Contribute your expertise to the professional learning communities.

Principle 3 objectives

Principle 3 of the NBPTS requires knowledge of staffing requirements.
- One of the goals is to adequately staff the library media center program by an accurate assessment of the student and teacher population, the goals of the school district, state requirements, and the amount and type of information materials collected in the media center.
- A second objective is to meet the information needs of students and faculty and other member of the school learning community. By being thoroughly cognizant of the demand for information, the library media specialist will advocate for suitable staffing levels to achieve that goal.
- Collaborate with library staff to meet the professional community and student needs.
- The certified librarian teacher must supervise media center staff.
- A final goal is to create accessibility to the community of students and faculty who use the media center.

Principle 4 objectives

Library goals cannot be achieved without the support of the school principal and other administrative officials. Principle 4 of NBCT recommends that the library media specialist teacher reach out to collaborate with school administrators in furtherance of information needs objectives.
- The media specialist-teacher must regularly communicate with the principal and others about planned activities and assessments of library operation.
- The media specialist must work with budget planners to ensure adequate financing for the media center's programs.

Copyright © Mometrix Media. You have been licensed one copy of this document for personal use only. Any other reproduction or redistribution is strictly prohibited. All rights reserved.

- The media center specialist should seek the support of the principal in the development of assessment criteria.
- The media specialist teacher should ally with the principal and other administrators to obtain support from social, professional, and governmental agencies outside of the immediate district.

Obtaining outside support

- The National Board Certified Teacher-Media Specialist should advance the goals of the media center by reaching out for support to organizations in the larger community. In order to do that, the library media specialist may do the following:The organizations, agencies, and community groups which would be useful for a partnership program advancing curriculum literacy goals. Community leaders and school administrators who may be of assistance in advancing information needs of the school and media center. Develop an information package which may be sent as a method of approach.
- Implement a strategy for linking public, university, and other school libraries to your local media center through both personal contact and through the 'information highway'.

ALA and internet filtering

The ALA position on internet filtering decries censorship and advises against software filtering mechanisms which block web sites. There are two basic types of internet filtering software. There are those which block a site by 'keyword' blocking and those which are set to block specific sites. The ALA position is grounded in the following concerns:
- The ALA notes that filters 'underblock and overblock' and that, in doing so, they limit the expression of protected free speech.
- The ALA notes that filters provide a false sense of security to parents. Filters are not able to block contact with children from pedophiles and other predators. Children should be educated with regard to the internet, the ALA believes, and that is the best form of protection against sexual predation.

Target groups

A primary goal of library media specialists is to create a friendly information environment which will encourage use of the facility. The image of the facility that the user takes away is an important part of library management and maintenance. There are five chief target groups which must be engaged in formulating a strategy: students, faculty, parents, administrators, and community groups and organizations.
There are many simple solutions to engagement of these groups which are often overlooked:
- Clean and maintain the physical plant. Engage the custodial staff in creating an environment that smells clean and is clean. Keep plants alive, replace light bulbs when they're burned out, remove clutter.
- Be sure that the media center support staff and volunteers projects a bright, positive image. Don't tolerate negative, unhelpful attitudes, and make it clear that service to the user group should be provided with sincerity and a sense of purpose.

Public relations actvities

The library media center specialist should energize an ongoing advocacy program.

Copyright © Mometrix Media. You have been licensed one copy of this document for personal use only. Any other reproduction or redistribution is strictly prohibited. All rights reserved.

- Conduct a Spring Reading Session inviting members of the community to read to the children. This is an ideal way of letting the taxpayers see exactly where their tax revenues are being spent.
- Write periodic press releases to the local newspapers informing them of ongoing activities, awards, or initiatives. Invite 'Op-Ed' people from the local papers to visit the media center as a way to keep them informed of technology initiatives and needs.
- Schedule informational meetings with community leaders and school board members in the media center facility.
- Be sure to include the library web page address and other relevant information in the periodic school newspaper or information bulletins.

Assessment activities and goals

Assessment is important not only as a measurement of achievement, it is also a litmus test for future planning and strategies. The goals of the media specialist teacher in the area of assessment are:
- Remain current with changing technology and educational strategies by participation in professional organizations, reading educational journals, and other methods of appraising assessment tools.
- Collaboration with other faculty and administrators is always important and should have many inputs.
- Apply different assessments to the different components of media center operation. Use traditional testing methods with students, and surveys with collaborative faculty and administration, for example.
- Use both qualitative and quantitative methods of assessment.
- Revise strategies based on information obtained through assessment, and provide reliable and consistent reports to the principal, faculty, and other administrators.

Leadership achievements

Standard Five of National Board Certification process refers to 'leading innovation through the library media program'. The national board can point to solid progress in this area. The School Library Journal reported the following in its study of LMS leadership initiatives:
- Eight-five percent of respondents to the study indicated that they were involved in continuing advocacy for library media program objectives.
- Three-fourths of the survey group reported that they participated in staff development activities, taught in-service workshops, or served as mentors for new teachers or library media specialists.
- A majority of library media specialists reported success in obtaining approved school board policies for selecting and evaluating collections.

Data versus information

One of the biggest problems with internet search engines is the great mass of material under each topical headline chosen by a user. This presents a particular problem for student researchers and for library media specialists trying to teach information literacy.
- Data is the mass body of snippets and headlines returned by search engines like Yahoo or Google. Some of the information returned may be useful but it is difficult to find in the

Copyright © Mometrix Media. You have been licensed one copy of this document for personal use only. Any other reproduction or redistribution is strictly prohibited. All rights reserved.

vast amount of data returned in a search. Other data returned from a search may be completely useless. Advertisers frequently flag their products under topical names which are commonly used in known searches.

- Information is useful data. Another way of saying that is the material returned by a search is relevant to the research topic. The library media specialist teaching information literacy must instruct students in the practice of extracting useful information from raw data.

Strategies for extracting information

There are several strategies the library media specialist may employ in teaching students how to extract useful information from the array of data which is returned by a general internet search. Some methods are more efficient than others.

- The use of free or subscription databases to reliable information sources is perhaps the easiest, and possibly the most expensive. Most states provide library subsidies so that they purchase subscriptions to online databases which specialize in research information. The gateways to such databases may be called by various names.
- In searching for useful information on the Wide Web, it is more practical to use 'deep web' search engines like iBoogie or Ixquick Metasearch than generalized search engines like Yahoo or Google.

Deep web search engine

So called 'deep web' search engines function in the same way as general search engines like Yahoo with one key difference. Deep web search engines engage in a 'clustering' process whereby the data is already grouped into useful categories.

'Clustering' is a process of assembling data objects by means of internal logarithms and presenting the results in a hierarchical form. Instead of having to look at an avalanche of raw data, the information seeker can pursue the paths most relevant to their information objectives. A search on the word 'milk may return 'clusters' of information grouped into various categories. One group may be about 'milk' in the category of 'dairy products'. Another category of 'milk' may be about 'health drinks'.

Clustering' is a process of grouping similar objects from a given set of inputs and presenting them in a hierarchy. Instead of having to look at an avalanche of raw data, the information seeker can pursue the paths most relevant to their information objectives. The search technology of a 'deep web' search engine uses algorithms or a set of search rules to sort data retrieved. There are two chief clustering techniques worthy of mentioning:

- 'Term extraction' is a necessary set of rules aimed at limiting inverted search data. Most internet users are familiar with searching a topic like 'Bill Johnson' and coming up with its inverse: 'Johnson Bill'. Term extraction is used to eliminate irrelevant data. The algorithm employed in this limiter is often called 'parsing'.
- Clustering has a final step after 'term extraction'. It uses a second set of algorithms which employ a combination of linguistics and statistics to general topical items grouped in useful hierarchies.

Alternative schools and literacy

Copyright © Mometrix Media. You have been licensed one copy of this document for personal use only. Any other reproduction or redistribution is strictly prohibited. All rights reserved.

Alternative schools have been defined in a variety of ways but one thing they have in common is special behaviors. In many cases, the special behaviors may have resulted from those students being removed from the public school environment. In other cases, a student may go to an alternative school by choice. Whatever the reason, the alternative school media specialist must adapt:

- Knowledge of learning styles and teaching techniques is useful in an alternative school where students may come from low socio-economic backgrounds, and have had problems with drugs, alcohol, and violent behavior.
- Bibliotherapy is a way of matching the media center collection to the youth of an alternative school. Materials in this collection may be directed at self-recognition and growth. The use of selective materials may assist alternative students in developing a positive identity.

Bibliotherapy

Bibliotherapy is just one mode of therapy in the vast area of educational psychology, but it is a term with which teachers and library media specialists should be familiar with.

- Bibliotherapy means the use of literature to guide human growth. For many students, it can open up areas of self-understanding, relieve frustration, and provide positive models of conflict resolution.
- The LMS or teacher employing bibliotherapy should be thoroughly familiar with any book used in this context. It is very important to match the book choice with the needs of the student population. Identity modeling and formation is a chief concern of middle and high school students.
- Group or open discussion of books should be planned in advance with areas of particular interest jotted down. This will prevent 'brain fade' when events force a change in methods and behavior.

Integration of instruction

Standard 4 of the National Board for Professional Teaching Standards focuses upon the objective of integration of instruction within all facets of the learning process. There are four key components to successful integration of the instructional process.

- Collaboration with curriculum teachers and developers makes the library media specialist a co-teacher in a process of developing curriculum and expanding information literacy.
- Planning is a large part of integration of the instructional process in a collaborative structure. Units of study in all subject areas must be developed in a way that combines information technology and research into a cohesive package.
- Implementation of information literacy goals and strategies is accomplished by the library media specialist who provides access to resources and technologies which enhance classroom learning.
- Assessment and measurement of performance activity is aimed at continuing the processes which work effectively and revising those which are less successful.

Proposition One

The National Board for Professional Teaching Standards grew out of an attempt to meet the information needs of students and professional communities of the 21st century. It relies upon five basic propositions as a foundation for developing its standards of information literacy.

Copyright © Mometrix Media. You have been licensed one copy of this document for personal use only. Any other reproduction or redistribution is strictly prohibited. All rights reserved.

Proposition One acknowledges that teacher commitment is a vital part of information literacy. The high standards required of the certified library media specialist teacher guarantee that information will flourish in a diverse cultural environment. The standard also recognizes that the teacher is the best guide for student self-realization and learning. Through ethical behavior and character modeling, the teacher can impart an appreciation of civic responsibility and ethical behavior.

Proposition Two

Proposition Two of the National Board Certification Standards takes the position that teachers and librarian teachers are most familiar with curriculum subject areas and learning methods. As experts in the field of cognition and human development as well as content areas, teachers are in the best position to guide students toward state and federal educational goals. Many of the challenges of the 21st century are in the area of technological innovation which has impacted both the outside world and the classroom. Teachers are best equipped to understand this and to implement strategies for knowledge growth. Teachers are familiar with 'skill gaps' and misconceptions which students bring to the classroom. As such, teacher are also expert in devising instructional techniques which are customized toward a diverse population.

Proposition Three

Proposition Three of the NBPTS mentions teacher management responsibility for student learning. Board Certified Teachers engage students, keeping them motivated when providing instruction and using their natural curiosity as a motivational component.
Teachers maintain a disciplined and protected environment which encourages learning. The classroom teacher and the library media specialist have acquired a broad base of behavioral knowledge which is applied to individual and group situations in the classroom.
Assessing individual and group progress is one of the teacher talents recognized by Proposition Three. This requires knowledge of a wide array of assessment techniques which form the basis of future instructional strategies.

Facilitating distance learning

Library media specialists can support distance learning by collaborating with curriculum designers and teachers in all stages of the planning process.
- Acting as a consultant on information delivery possibilities and limitations is just one important function of the library media specialist as the messenger of distance learning.
- Much of the library media specialist's participation in the delivery of distance learning will be through the acquisition of delivery technologies. Multiple copies of materials and sufficient equipment should be funded and acquired to extend the reach of learning to distance student populations.
- The LMS can expedite and enhance contact between teachers and students by arranging for teleconferencing sessions or by providing a meeting place and time in the media center. This requires a flexible schedule and a current knowledge of technological innovations. The increasing use of podcast devices to deliver instructional content is an example of a comparatively inexpensive delivery innovation.

Humanistic learning theory

Copyright © Mometrix Media. You have been licensed one copy of this document for personal use only.
Any other reproduction or redistribution is strictly prohibited. All rights reserved.

Humanistic psychology and social science is deeply imbedded into learning theory. The humanistic theories of learning allow for the subjective aspects of student behavior. Within this concept of student learning, feelings of the student are as important as rational thinking and programmed behavior. Adherents to this style of learning believe that cognitive functioning will be inhibited unless the teacher takes basic emotional needs into account. The theory posits self-actualization as the end goal of learning. Outward behavior and achievement is determined by engaging the learner in objectives involving self-actualization rather a set of external goals. In order for learning to take place, educational formulas must be relevant to the individual and have personal meaning for the student. SDL is a term often used for this type of learning. It means Self Directed Learning.

AECT policy rules

The policy statement of the Association for Educational Communication and Technology (AECT) is a set of guidelines which define ethical behavior in the use and management of educational technology:

- The media information center manager must be intellectually honest and able to separate personal views from institutional and organizational viewpoints.
- The media center manager must not use library facilities or resources for private financial gain, nor grant exceptions to users of the facility with a view to gaining favor with specific groups.
- The media center manager must not accept gifts in kind or otherwise from members of the public using the facility.
- The media center manager must not accept special favors from businesses selling products to the library or servicing the media center technologies.

Internet sources and bibliography

Not surprisingly, there is no general agreement on the format to be used for the citation of internet sources in research. There are some guidelines and conventions which are commonly used until a standard method is adopted.
Provide as much information as possible concerning the author of the source and its origin.

Adopt the format of conventional print sources as they are cited. The well-known APA style guidelines or the Chicago Style manual are frequently used as models for internet and web-based citations.
There are several style initiatives for internet citations and they are at various stages of development and acceptance: The Columbia guide to Online Style, and the Citation Guides of Electronic Documents are just two examples under development.

Important Terms

Phishing refers to the illegal practice of obtaining personal financial data by the construction of fraudulent website pages. Fraudulent 'phishing' pages resemble real and legitimate sites and encourage users to enter personal information into phony 'forms'.
File-sharing refers to peer-to-peer transfer of material sometimes without regard for copyright. There is an array of software and hardware products dedicated to file sharing between users.
RSS means Rich Site Summary, an XML format which is widely used on the internet. The advantage of RSS data transmission is that the use of this common language facilitates its manipulation and delivery by aggregation software. By the use of RSS and news aggregation software, website

Copyright © Mometrix Media. You have been licensed one copy of this document for personal use only. Any other reproduction or redistribution is strictly prohibited. All rights reserved.

content can be delivered and constantly updated within sites which are constructed to accept RSS 'feeds'.

VoIP is the acronym for Voice over Internet Protocol. It refers to technology which allows the use of a computer to transmit voice telephone calls over the internet to other users. VoIP software translates a telephone's analog signals to digital signals which can travel throughout the World Wide Web. VoIP has the advantage of bypassing conventional long-distance communication and is free.

Wi-Fi refers to wireless internet connections or 'wireless fidelity'. It uses a common standard IEEE.80211. This protocol allows computers and personal digital assistants to share an internet connection over various distances, usually from 300 to 700 feet. Later versions of the wi-fi protocol use the same standard specifications but are designated as "G" or "N" which allows connection from greater distances and at greater speeds. Installations of wireless networks are considerably less expensive than wired systems and, for this reason, they are becoming increasingly more popular in school libraries.

Bread-crumb trail structure is often used in the large and complex database sites which are often found in libraries. Previous web pages may be displayed on a single menu line. This allows the user to backtrack when necessary.

'Frames' refers to the use of a stationary page to launch other independently controllable pages simultaneously. Experienced users profit from the speed advantage obtained by having something to look at (and learn from) while secondary pages load.

Site Maps might be initially used to gain an overview of possible directions of navigation or research. Site maps can save considerable time when an internet user has a visual representation of possible choices and directions of search.

URL or Universal Resource Locator refers to the web address where a website may be found. Putting the URL in the open search window of a web browser will display the requested site.

Text File Extension: Following are some typical text file extensions: .txt; .wps; .xls; .doc. By recognizing text file extensions, the user may be able to identify a particular word processor, database, or spreadsheet composer which was used to create the file.

Graphic file extensions may include .bmp (bitmap); jpg (often called j-pegs); .gif (graphic interface file) and others. Recognizing these will allow the research to see pictures or other graphics if the software recognizes them and is compatible.

URL File Extensions: URLs have extensions, too. URL extensions (.com; .gov; .mil; .net; .org; .edu) are recognizable clues which provide immediate information about the source of online information.

A 'field' is one of the categories of division in a menu of information. Typical 'fields' in a library catalogue may include author, date of publication, type of material (book, film, CD-Rom), and title. A 'field' search allows the user to access the information by means of a chosen field.

A 'dynamic web page' is one that allows the user to 'interact' by generating information which flows from the user's request for information. Its opposite is a 'static' web page wherein information can only be obtained by following a link to subsequent (and different) web pages.

A 'Boolean operator' refers to the use of words like 'AND, OR, NOT) to narrow or limit an online search to certain conditions. Boolean operators sometimes consist of putting parentheses (.....) around search words to control the order of the search.

A 'full text' document contains the entire text in a document or article. Thousands of full-text articles have been digitized and can be accessed on computers, though they commonly lose graphics which may exist in the originals.

OPAC is the abbreviation for Online Public Access Catalog. It is the digital equivalent of the old card catalogue and contains location and other information about most of the materials the library may hold or lend.

Copyright © Mometrix Media. You have been licensed one copy of this document for personal use only. Any other reproduction or redistribution is strictly prohibited. All rights reserved.

PDF files are converted from their original form, usually in one of the many word processing applications on the market, to a common form which is available to all. The protocol was developed by Adobe systems which allows free download of the PDF file reader. PDF files eliminate the conflicts caused by materials written with different word processing applications.

Co-Planning is a fundamental and necessary activity in integrating instruction into the overall curriculum.   The National Board Certified Teacher should become familiar with all aspects of the curriculum in order to be a partner with the teacher in the planning process.   Teacher and library media specialist, both certified and capable, must exchange ideas, and then turn ideas into action.

Co-Teaching is the process and implementation of plans and ideas. The NBCT and the library media specialist will be equal partners in accomplishing the learning task.   Schedules will be arranged toward goal achievement, and for the accommodation of student learning activities.   The classroom and the library will both be focal points of connected learning activity.

Co-Assessment means that the classroom teacher and the library media specialist contribute equally to the mosaic of student evaluation in content and information literacy.

Copyright © Mometrix Media. You have been licensed one copy of this document for personal use only.
Any other reproduction or redistribution is strictly prohibited. All rights reserved.

Practice Test

Practice Questions

1. A librarian sees that a third grade student's checked-out book is two months overdue. Several overdue notices have already been given to the student's teacher to give to him. Which of the following would be the best action for the librarian to take now?
   a. The next time the class comes in for its library period, call that student's name and ask him in front of his classmates where the book is, why he has not returned it, and when he plans to do so.
   b. Call the parents and ask them to help the student return the book.
   c. Inform the principal that disciplinary action is called for because the student has ignored the overdue notices.
   d. Give the student a "lost book" bill for the entire value of the book.

2. A librarian wants to have a fund-raising book fair. Which of the following should be her first course of action?
   a. Announce the book fair in the school newsletter.
   b. Survey teachers for the types of books they would like to see at the book fair.
   c. Check with the principal to be sure of the school calendar and any school or district guidelines for fundraising activities.
   d. Ask students what kind of books they would like to buy at a book fair.

3. A new librarian discovers that her predecessor shelved all the "easy-to-read" books for younger children on the lowest shelves near the floor. What should she do about this, if anything?
   a. Provide comfortable pillows on the floor for students to sit or kneel on as they search for books.
   b. Remind primary students where these books are located so that they can easily access them.
   c. Inventory these books to determine if they are age-appropriate.
   d. Move the collection to higher shelves.

4. Which of the following is NOT a professional association for librarians?
   a. Texas Association of School Librarians
   b. American Library Association
   c. American Association of School Librarians
   d. American Union of Library Employees

5. Which of the following criteria should be used when "weeding" books from a library's collection?
   a. The book contains material that is outdated or inaccurate.
   b. The book contains subject matter that is controversial.
   c. Students do not check out the book very often.
   d. Parent organizations have requested that the book be removed.

Copyright © Mometrix Media. You have been licensed one copy of this document for personal use only. Any other reproduction or redistribution is strictly prohibited. All rights reserved.

6. A new librarian in an elementary school wants to move the library schedule from fixed to flexible. How should she go about doing this in order to obtain the greatest cooperation from staff members?

    a. Discuss with the principal the educational advantages and also the financial aspects of a flexible schedule. Flexible scheduling may require the hiring of a library assistant, for example. Offer to make the transition gradually so that the school budget for flexible library scheduling can be increased little by little.

    b. Involve teachers in planning for the change. Ask about their curricular and library needs. While the schedule is still fixed, ask teachers to stay when they bring their classes and help teach a coordinated lesson.

    c. Begin with a mixed schedule, where some classes, such as kindergartners, come for their weekly "story time," while classes from higher grades visit the library as needed.

    d. All of the above

7. A librarian would use the MARC system when:

    a. When deciding what outdated or damaged books need to be weeded from the collection.

    b. When cataloging new books for the library collection.

    c. When deciding the best arrangement for books on the library shelves.

    d. When creating a library budget for the following year.

8. A librarian observes that a teacher has made 35 copies of the first page of a 7-page science article in a magazine, one copy for each of his students. He states that he has cleared this with the principal. Are the teacher's actions allowable under copyright law?

    a. Yes, under the Fair Usage provision of the copyright law.

    b. No, because only a single copy may be made of copyrighted material.

    c. Yes, because the teacher obtained permission from the principal to make these copies.

    d. No, because by copying the article, the teacher denies the author financial gain from his or her work.

9. Which of the following is the best way for a librarian to demonstrate respect for diversity in a school with a large population of Hispanic and Asian students?

    a. During library instruction, the librarian should repeatedly ask students if they understand her to make sure that students for whom English is a second language are receiving instruction that they understand.

    b. Create a display of books and other materials on ethnic topics and invite students and parents to visit one evening and browse the display. Then, have a discussion period during which parents and children are invited to share special aspects of their heritages and customs.

    c. Budget for books and media materials in Spanish, Chinese, Vietnamese, Korean, and Japanese at a variety of reading levels and on a variety of subjects.

    d. When classes come for their assigned library time, ask students of various heritages to identify themselves and tell the class (in English) about their customs and languages.

Copyright © Mometrix Media. You have been licensed one copy of this document for personal use only. Any other reproduction or redistribution is strictly prohibited. All rights reserved.

10. Which would be the most appropriate way for a librarian to instruct students in Internet research skills?

    a. Assign classes that come for their library period to choose a topic, locate information on the Internet and write down the website where they located it. When time is up, the librarian should call classes together to share.

    b. Prepare a Power Point presentation that demonstrates the process of locating information on the Internet and present this program to all classes that come to the library.

    c. After conferring with each classroom teacher about his or her current curriculum, demonstrate separately to different classes how to use the Internet to find information on the topic each class is presently studying.

    d. Prepare a display of books about using the Internet and use class time to show these books to students, urging them to check out the books and read for themselves about ways to find information online.

11. A teacher asks the school librarian to find a specific book she needs for a lesson she is preparing. After consulting MARC records, the librarian determines that this particular book is not in her collection. What is the best choice she can make under these circumstances?

    a. Use her budget and immediately buy a copy of the book.

    b. Suggest an alternate resource to the teacher.

    c. Obtain the book through interlibrary loan.

    d. Apologize and suggest that the teacher consult the local public library.

12. All of the following are good ways that a librarian can raise funds for the library EXCEPT:

    a. Applying for a grant.

    b. Having a book fair.

    c. Asking for funds from the Parents Association.

    d. Soliciting paid advertising to run on the library's website.

13. Before creating a statement of standards for her media center, a librarian should first

    a. Ask the principal what standards to use.

    b. Ask librarians in other districts what standards they have used.

    c. Research all applicable national, state, and district standards.

    d. Call the superintendent's office and ask permission to create a library standards statement.

14. What is the best way a librarian can assist a classroom teacher who has assigned a history research project to his class?

    a. Offer to visit the classroom and teach part of the lesson.

    b. Offer students a small reward for the best completed research project.

    c. Demonstrate to the class how to use the library's computers for research.

    d. Direct students to areas of the library that deal with history.

Copyright © Mometrix Media. You have been licensed one copy of this document for personal use only. Any other reproduction or redistribution is strictly prohibited. All rights reserved.

15. A librarian has just purchased new software for the library's computers that will make research easier and more effective. After the software is installed and she has become familiar with it, what should she do next?
    a. Hold a brief staff meeting to instruct teachers and library staff in using the new software.
    b. Circulate a memo explaining the changes and how to use the new software.
    c. Instruct each class that comes to the library about how to use the new software.
    d. As students enter the library to do research on the computer, instruct them individually about how to use the new software.

16. A librarian observes a student working at a computer who moves rapidly from on website to another, apparently having difficulty locating material. The best way for the librarian to help this student would be to:
    a. Ask the student what she is looking for and then locate the proper information for her.
    b. Wait for the student to become frustrated and ask for the librarian's help.
    c. Ask the student if he or she would like some help and abide by the student's response.
    d. Step forward and demonstrate to the student how to find an appropriate website.

17. In selecting new books for an elementary school library's collection, which of the following would be the librarian's best resource?
    a. Journals such as The Horn Book
    b. Magazines such as Atlantic Monthly: Books & Critics
    c. Newspapers such as The New York Times Book Review
    d. Online resources such as MAA Reviews

18. Which of the following technological duties would NOT be part of the librarian's job description?
    a. Housing and maintaining computer labs
    b. Producing the daily televised school announcements
    c. Monitoring student use of cell phones
    d. Maintaining the school's website

Question 19 to 21 pertain to the following information:
        A school librarian is preparing her first monthly report to the principal. She is new to both this school and to her job.

19. Before beginning her report, the librarian should do all of the following EXCEPT:
    a. Review monthly library reports from the previous year.
    b. Check with her administrator to find out if there is a required format for monthly reports.
    c. Consider ways to make the report more meaningful and design a new format.
    d. Collect statistics on circulation, library classes, and computer and copier usage.

20. What kind of statistics should be included in the librarian's monthly report to the principal?
    a. Circulation statistics
    b. The number of individual and class visits to the library
    c. Usage of technology, including computers, data bases, printers, copiers
    d. All of the above

Copyright © Mometrix Media. You have been licensed one copy of this document for personal use only. Any other reproduction or redistribution is strictly prohibited. All rights reserved.

21. In a library media center that follows a flexible schedule, it is important for the librarian's monthly report to include what other kinds of information besides statistics?
    a. Problems with staff and students
    b. Collaborative projects with teachers
    c. Future plans for library growth
    d. Budget requests

22. The Online Public Access Catalog (OPAC) is a technological improvement of and a replacement for:
    a. The MARC system
    b. The card catalog
    c. The Dewey Decimal system
    d. The Readers' Guide to Periodical Literature

23. You have an opportunity to invite a published author of children's books to spend a day in your school library visiting with students. What is the best reason to give for this visit when discussing this idea with your principal?
    a. The visit will be good PR for the school. The media can be advised of the visit.
    b. The visit will contribute to literature appreciation for all students.
    c. Opportunities will be provided to sell the author's books so that he can autograph them. This can be a fundraising activity for the library.
    d. Students may check out some of his books, adding to the circulation statistics for the month.

24. A librarian is aware that students in one of her classes come from several different cultural backgrounds, and some do not speak or understand English well. She wants to have this group do some research on the Internet under her guidance. To be sure that the ESL students understand and are able to complete this assignment successfully, what is the librarian's best course of action?
    a. Ask the teacher not to bring these students with the rest of the class. Arrange another time to instruct them individually or in small groups.
    b. Have students work on the assignment in pairs or small groups. Assign students to groups in which each struggling ESL student will have a partner to help him or her understand and complete the assignment. Encourage groups or pairs to ask for help as needed.
    c. Explain the assignment to the whole class in simple words, speaking slowly so that everyone can understand. Have students work independently.
    d. Write the directions for the assignment and give them to students. Include diagrams that demonstrate what students are expected to do.

25. You observe a student at the computer cutting and pasting material from an online article into his own report. What is the best way to handle this situation?
    a. Pretend you did not notice, but notify the teacher who assigned the report.
    b. Quietly discuss with the student the rules about plagiarism, show him ways to put the information in his own words, and ask to see his report when he has rewritten it.
    c. Send the student to the principal for a serious infraction of library and school rules.
    d. Arrange a meeting between the student, the teacher who assigned the report, and the student's parents to discuss the student's plagiarism.

Copyright © Mometrix Media. You have been licensed one copy of this document for personal use only. Any other reproduction or redistribution is strictly prohibited. All rights reserved.

26. Which activities below would it be best for a beginning librarian NOT to engage in right after arriving at a new school?
    a. Weeding and schedule changing
    b. Staff meetings on preventing plagiarism
    c. Fund raising activities such as book fairs
    d. Reorganizing the library furniture

27. Why is it a good educational idea for the librarian to have a "story time" for younger students in elementary school?
    a. It frees the classroom teacher for a prep period.
    b. The librarian can model proper library behavior.
    c. During story time, the librarian can teach students word recognition skills.
    d. Hearing stories read aloud contributes to students' interest in reading.

28. A school district is forming a committee of teachers to create a new curriculum guide for the teaching of middle school Language Arts. What is the strongest argument for including the school librarian on that committee?
    a. Knowing about changes to the curriculum and participating in making those changes will enable the librarian to acquire materials that support the new curriculum.
    b. As a professional educator, the librarian should be a member of all school committees.
    c. The librarian may have more knowledge than teachers about state curriculum requirements in the area of Language Arts.
    d. Librarians have a more global approach to curriculum than teachers.

29. A weekly block of library time is assigned to a seventh grade class in a middle school. The librarian could best use this time with students by
    a. Instructing them in effective ways to do research on the Internet and in efficient use of library reference materials and books on the library bookshelves.
    b. Allowing this time to be a "free" period for students when they can return books, select others, and ask the librarian for help and guidance when they see a need for it.
    c. Introducing them to new materials in the library's collection by reading short passages from new books and showing brief previews of new DVDs and audio books.
    d. Asking them to be "library aides" during this period so that they can assist younger students who are looking for materials and also reshelf books.

30. Early in the school year, a school librarian sends a survey to classroom teachers asking for topics and tentative dates they plan to teach those topics in their curriculum this year. What should be the librarian's response to the information received in the survey?
    a. In a school with a fixed schedule, the librarian will plan instruction in ways to research these topics on the appropriate dates when she meets with those classes.
    b. In a school with flexible scheduling, the librarian will suggest that teachers sign up to bring classes to the library when they begin a new topic.
    c. The librarian will pull material from the collection and loan the teacher a cart of appropriate research materials to use in the classroom at the time of each project.
    d. All of the above

Copyright © Mometrix Media. You have been licensed one copy of this document for personal use only. Any other reproduction or redistribution is strictly prohibited. All rights reserved.

31. Before the first day of school, a librarian organizes her library. Which of these concepts of library design is most important
   a. Seating students apart from each other and facing a blank wall so that nothing around them is distracting.
   b. Providing small chairs and tables for younger students and larger furniture for older students.
   c. Organizing space into areas that can be flexibly arranged to accommodate different sizes of groups as well as community activities held after school.
   d. Arranging groups of chairs and computer stations so that no one is out of the librarian's sight while she is checking out books.

32. According to state guidelines, the walls of the school library should display:
   a. Posters reminding students to be quiet
   b. The school calendar for the year
   c. Student-produced work
   d. Materials created by the librarian

33. Which of the following is a good way to ensure that library use extends beyond the school day and involves families and the community?
   a. Invite one or two classes for an hour-long after-school activity related to their area of study.
   b. Have an open house in the library once a month and invite families to browse the library's collection and get to know the librarian.
   c. Announce a plan to keep the library open one day a week for an hour after school so that students can do research.
   d. Email parents with a schedule that offers time in the library after school for certain families on certain dates.

34. The librarian is aware of students' different learning styles and addresses them in his/her instruction by:
   a. Using a variety of instructional techniques that actively involve students in listening, working with various media and materials, reading, and writing.
   b. Dividing students into groups based on their learning styles and instructing each group separately.
   c. Devoting more time to those students who have trouble grasping ideas or reading different kinds of material while the rest of the group waits.
   d. None of the above

35. A school librarian wants to keep families and the community informed about what is happening in the school media center. A good way to accomplish this is by:
   a. Creating a web page where students, families, and community members can find information about the library's current activities and upcoming events.
   b. Emailing parents periodically to keep them updated.
   c. Publishing a monthly newsletter that students can take home and that can also be sent electronically to local media outlets.
   d. All of the above

Copyright © Mometrix Media. You have been licensed one copy of this document for personal use only. Any other reproduction or redistribution is strictly prohibited. All rights reserved.

36. A teacher is having his class research the Civil Rights movement of the 1960s. He wants his students to perform an Internet search, but as librarian, you know that some of the sites that would help the students have been blocked by the school district's filter that prevents students from going to inappropriate sites. You arrange for the technology department to remove the block on the sites the history class will use, make a list of those sites, and give the list to the teacher. Which of the following reasons would you cite as justification for what you have done?
   a. The Patriot Act of 2001
   b. The No Child Left Behind Act of 2002
   c. An Acceptable Use Policy
   d. MARC records

37. A Boolean library search involves
   a. Mathematical input to narrow the search area
   b. Using keywords with "or," "but," or "and"
   c. Accessing a special information database
   d. Using the Dewey Decimal System

38. Which of the following is NOT a responsibility of a school librarian?
   a. Scheduling classes
   b. Reporting statistics to administrators
   c. Circulating library materials
   d. Critiquing books

39. A teacher has brought his class to the library for instruction and book exchange. The teacher participates in the instructional session with the librarian, but when students are excused to look for books and disperse to different areas in the library, the teacher ignores their behavior. Two boys are chasing each other around a shelf of books. The teacher does not correct them. What should the librarian do?
   a. Point out the behavior to the teacher.
   b. Ignore the behavior.
   c. Speak to the boys firmly about proper library behavior.
   d. Call for the principal to handle the problem.

40. The library has been granted funding for a paid media clerk to assist the librarian. Hiring and supervising this clerk will be the librarian's responsibility. What is the first action the librarian should take?
   a. Advertise the position in the local newspaper.
   b. Draw up a complete job description of the position.
   c. Call up friends who might want to take the job.
   d. Research how other librarians use media clerks.

41. A librarian wants to weed the library's book collection. How should she go about doing this?
   a. Cancel classes and spend a school day alone weeding the materials.
   b. After library hours are over, stay late and weed the materials.
   c. Form a committee of interested teachers to help weed the collection at a time that is convenient for everyone.
   d. Invite students to select the books they use and like the least and weed those first.

Copyright © Mometrix Media. You have been licensed one copy of this document for personal use only. Any other reproduction or redistribution is strictly prohibited. All rights reserved.

42. Which of the following activities encourages students to read and enjoy reading?
    a. A school book fair
    b. Reading contests such as Battle of the Books
    c. School book clubs
    d. All of the above

Questions 43 and 44 pertain to the following situation:
    A student comes to the library and you observe him wandering confusedly in the library's section of science books.

43. What is the first thing you should do to help him?
    a. Ask the student what his assignment is and what kind of books he is looking for.
    b. Tell the student that books are shelved by the author's last name and let him have the opportunity to use this information to find the books he is looking for.
    c. Find an opportunity later on to ask his teacher what the assignment is so that if he has difficulty locating materials the next time he comes to the library, you can help him.
    d. Send another student from his class over to help him, as they both have the same assignment.

44. You interview the student and he tells you that he has been assigned to write a paper on the annual migration of Monarch butterflies from North America to Mexico. Which of the following would you suggest that the student do first?
    a. Look for books in the Dewey Decimal System with the number 590, Zoology.
    b. Put "butterflies" into an Internet search engine.
    c. Use OPAC to find MARC entries about Monarch butterfly migration.
    d. Consult the Readers' Guide to Periodical Literature for articles on the topic.

45. Which of the following is the LEAST effective way to involve parents in library programs?
    a. Put a notice in the school newsletter asking for parent volunteers to help in the library.
    b. Write about what is going on in the library in your school newsletter and invite parents to visit the library on both a drop-in basis and at a scheduled parents' night.
    c. Send a note home with students inviting parents to a "parents' night" at the library.
    d. Put a notice on the school website that parents are invited to "parents' night" at the library.

46. A new school librarian is having difficulty getting everything done on time. Which of the following would be the BEST first step for her to take to solve her problem?
    a. Supervise the media clerk more closely and assign that person more tasks.
    b. Ask the principal to hire more help in the library than the library has traditionally had.
    c. Make comprehensive daily, weekly, and monthly plans listing what needs to be done, the deadline for completing each task, and the person responsible for handling the task.
    d. Put in overtime hours as necessary to complete all tasks on time.

Copyright © Mometrix Media. You have been licensed one copy of this document for personal use only. Any other reproduction or redistribution is strictly prohibited. All rights reserved.

47. A new librarian discovers that her predecessor had a fixed-schedule program that allowed classes to visit the library at assigned times every week, leaving little time open for other activities. The library did not host specials events such as book fairs, Battle of the Books, student reading clubs, etc. The new librarian's vision for her media center includes all these activities, as well as flexible scheduling to allow students more individual library time. What is the FIRST step she should take to accomplish these goals?
    a. Announce her plans for flexible scheduling at the next staff meeting and implement them immediately. Time should not be wasted on outdated kinds of schedules.
    b. Discuss her plans for change with the principal and get his/her input about the concept and affordability of flexible scheduling, as well as potential costs to the library in hosting special events.
    c. Do nothing at the present because the staff and principal seem very content with the way the library functioned in the past and postpone the idea until next year.
    d. Discuss with teachers, either at a staff meeting or individually, the advantages of flexible scheduling and plan to begin a flexible program with a few classes from each grade.

48. Which of the following would be an effective way for a librarian to share her goals for the media center with district officials and the school administration?
    a. Draw up a comprehensive statement of goals and visions for the media center.
    b. Speak at a meeting of the school board and explain the goals for the media center.
    c. Schedule a meeting with the principal to discuss implementing those goals.
    d. All of the above

49. Which of the following best explains the difference between hardware and software?
    a. Hardware is a program like Adobe Acrobat installed on the computer using a CD or DVD. Software refers to programs already on the computer when it is purchased.
    b. Hardware is a physical component of a computer, such as a monitor, RAM, CPU, hard drive, or motherboard. Software is a series of coded instructions that direct the computer to perform certain operations.
    c. Hardware includes the basic operating system of a computer, such as Windows Vista. Software refers to components of that system such as RAM and ROM.
    d. Hardware is the security system of a computer, such as a firewall or virus protection. Software consists of programs on the computer that are vulnerable to viruses.

50. Which of the following would NOT be an effective way to communicate information to parents?
    a. A Power Point presentation to the parents' association meeting
    b. A telephone call to each family
    c. A newsletter sent to each family
    d. Teleconferencing with groups of parents at a time

Copyright © Mometrix Media. You have been licensed one copy of this document for personal use only. Any other reproduction or redistribution is strictly prohibited. All rights reserved.

51. The school librarian has been invited to address a luncheon meeting of the local Kiwanis Club, an organization of business people. In order to do this, she will need to get the   principal's permission. She will also need to arrange for release time, since the luncheon   lasts much longer than school lunch period. She will have to prepare her talk, and to design and make copies of a handout about the media center to give the Kiwanis members. Will the media center or the school benefit if the librarian accepts this invitation, or should she politely reject it?

    a. The librarian should accept the invitation because business people can support the media center in several ways, including donating computers, giving money for library projects, and supporting the goals and visions of the librarian and her school. By attending the luncheon, the librarian will create good will for the school and the library.

    b. There is really no point in the librarian going to this much trouble to speak to a small group of business people. There is no way they can provide direct help to the library or to the school, and her time is precious. She should politely turn down the invitation or have her principal reject the invitation for her. This kind of activity is not within the job description of a school librarian.

    c. She should attend the meeting and speak out of a sense of community obligation but should not expect anything productive from giving a speech at a luncheon meeting of business people. They invite a speaker every month and probably do not pay careful attention to whatever the speaker discusses. They will most likely be focused more on the food than on the content of her speech.

    d. The librarian should not speak to this group because they may have a political agenda she is unaware of. For example, they may want to ban some books from the library or may feel that the library is over-funded. When these businesspeople were in school, the library had a card catalogue and no computers. They will be likely to think that what was good enough then should be good enough now. Their minds may be made up, and her speech is not likely to change their attitudes.

52. What are the advantages of getting to know public librarians and academic librarians in your area?

    a. You can send students to these libraries to check out books they need.

    b. You may exchange information from each other's databases.

    c. These librarians may have children in your school.

    d. The public and academic libraries may have collections you want to own.

53. As books and supplies are received by the library, what is the first step the librarian should take?

    a. Paste labels giving required information on the spines of the books.

    b. Decide where on the library shelves the new materials should be placed.

    c. Stamp them with the name of the library/media center.

    d. Check the items received against the purchase orders.

54. Why should the librarian periodically review online databases?

    a. To make sure students are not plagiarizing from them

    b. To verify that the subject matter is accurate and covers student needs

    c. To make sure nothing inappropriate for students is on the database

    d. To assess the difficulty of the reading levels on the database

Copyright © Mometrix Media. You have been licensed one copy of this document for personal use only. Any other reproduction or redistribution is strictly prohibited. All rights reserved.

55. A lesson given by the librarian to staff and/or students on creating Power Point presentations should include all of the following EXCEPT:
    a. Design
    b. Content Delivery
    c. Audience
    d. Bibliography

56. Inviting a writer into the library for a day or a week to work with children on their own writing and encourage them in their reading should have all the following direct outcomes EXCEPT:
    a. Encourage student interest in reading and writing
    b. Raise money for library needs and projects.
    c. Increase the number of books checked out by students
    d. Demonstrate through a successful role model that being a reader/writer is desirable

57. The librarian creates a computer "scavenger hunt." Students work at computers to find items on a list of computer resources. The first student to successfully find all the items and write down the websites where they are located is declared the winner, the "Champion Computer Researcher." This activity promotes which of the following state goals for library media centers?
    a. The ethical use of information resources
    b. The appreciation of diversity within a student group
    c. Effective oral and written communication
    d. Integrating technology into the library program

58. A school librarian has an opportunity to help promote a proposed state law which would increase funding for school libraries, specifically in the area of granting funds for more technology in those libraries. She would have to make phone calls to voters and appear on TV to promote the library's technological needs. What should she do?
    a. She should turn down the opportunity because public school employees are not supposed to get involved in politics.
    b. She should limit her support activities to handing out flyers to her students to take home to their families, urging them to vote for the measure.
    c. She should accept the opportunity but make phone calls to voters and give television interviews on her own time.
    d. She should campaign only to her own school staff, urging them to vote for the measure.

59. A school librarian is cooperating with other librarians in the district to write a Fair Use Policy for the district that will be applied to all schools. Which of the following should NOT be included in that policy?
    a. The conditions under which copies may be made of published material
    b. The length of time any one student may be allowed to spend on the Internet
    c. Guidelines for student access to the Internet, including whether or not students may have email accounts
    d. Penalties for violations of the Fair Use Policy, especially as it pertains to plagiarism

Copyright © Mometrix Media. You have been licensed one copy of this document for personal use only. Any other reproduction or redistribution is strictly prohibited. All rights reserved.

60. A teacher approaches the school librarian with a lesson plan in Language Arts that will involve student research use several types of sources, including encyclopedias, biographies, and the Internet. How can the librarian best help the teacher achieve the goals of the lesson plan?

  a. Ask the teacher to give students the assignment and then schedule a time to bring the class to the library. Directly teach students research techniques for print materials and for the Internet. Show them how to locate internet databases that will meet their needs and how to coordinate information from several sources.

  b. Give the teacher a list of appropriate databases, show her where biographies and encyclopedias are shelved in the library, and ask her to schedule a time for her class to come in and do their research under her supervision.

  c. Schedule a time to visit the teacher's classroom and answer any questions students may have about doing this type of research.

  d. All of the above

61. A teacher is concerned that some students in his class who were researching a topic on the Internet found some biased, incorrect information and unknowingly included it in their reports. What is the first action the librarian should take to prevent this from happening again?

  a. Have a staff meeting to discuss the problem of unreliable resources that may be biased. Ask teachers to help solve this problem.

  b. Obtain a list of suspect databases from the concerned teacher and evaluate each one carefully to see if the information is accurate, reliable, and unbiased. Remove these sources from the library's collection.

  c. Ask the concerned teacher to visit the websites himself and report to the librarian his opinion of the information he finds there.

  d. In your next period with this class, explain how to examine information obtained from the Internet for accuracy.

62. A librarian is drawing up a plan for a lesson on creating a Power Point presentation. The class she is going to instruct contains several students for whom English is a second language. What is the best way for the librarian to handle the potential difficulties these students may have in understanding her?

  a. She should inform these students that if they feel they will not understand what she is saying, they are excused from the lesson and may spend the time browsing the library's collection.

  b. Since Power Point is a visual medium, she should take advantage of that and show what to do rather than lecturing about it. She can invite students to try some of the techniques she is teaching and make the lesson as hands-on as possible so that its content will cross the language barrier.

  c. She should assign each ESL student a student partner who will sit with them and help explain what she is saying.

  d. When she gives her lecture, she should speak very slowly and clearly and periodically stop to ask for anyone who does not understand the lesson to raise his or her hand.

Copyright © Mometrix Media. You have been licensed one copy of this document for personal use only. Any other reproduction or redistribution is strictly prohibited. All rights reserved.

63. Several parents have volunteered to work in the library. The librarian wants to talk to all of them to find out what hours and days they have free and what kind of volunteer work they want to do. What is the most efficient way to gather this information and cause the least disruption to the potential volunteers?
  a. Call each volunteer individually on the phone.
  b. Send each volunteer an email and ask for email response.
  c. Use teleconferencing so that they all can exchange information at the same time.
  d. Ask the volunteers to attend an after-school volunteers' meeting.

64. Which of the following is an advantage of the OPAC system?
  a. Patrons can find materials easily.
  b. Libraries can track what materials are checked out.
  c. OPAC is an aid to purchasing and cataloging material.
  d. All of the above

65. A teacher wants to display the maps and models her students created during a geography unit. She approaches the librarian and asks if it would be appropriate to display them in the library. How should the librarian respond?
  a. The librarian should say that geography is not related to English, reading, or literature, which are the library's primary goals and therefore not appropriate for library display.
  b. The librarian should say that she has decorated the walls the way she wants them to remain during the school year, and it would be too much trouble to take them down for the teacher's display.
  c. The librarian should say that children in other classes might become jealous if one class's material is on display and their own work is not.
  d. The librarian should say that she will be happy to help organize a display of students' geography projects. After all, they did their geography research in the library. Other students will be inspired when they see the results of classroom work and library research.

66. A librarian receives a letter from a group that objects to a particular book in the school library. The group asks to have the book removed from the library's shelves. The librarian discusses the problem with her principal, who asks her to inform the group that in accordance with the selection policy adopted by the school district, the book will remain on the library shelves. What is the best form for her response to the protesting group to take?
  a. Oral, in the form of a phone call to the leader of the complaining group
  b. Written, in the form of a letter to the group
  c. Electronic, in the form of an e-mail
  d. Non-verbal, no reply is given to the letter but a copy of the selection policy is sent to the complaining group

67. When a school librarian is deciding to add to the library's collection, what is the first step she should take?
  a. Create a written five-year collection plan.
  b. Study the catalogs of the library's usual providers.
  c. Evaluate the current collection and note any areas that lack materials.
  d. Discuss adding to the collection with the principal.

Copyright © Mometrix Media. You have been licensed one copy of this document for personal use only. Any other reproduction or redistribution is strictly prohibited. All rights reserved.

68. A school librarian gives every student in the elementary school a book to read over the summer. In what ways will this help students?
    a. Students will maintain their reading skills.
    b. Students will develop further interest in and knowledge of age-appropriate literature.
    c. Students will engage in a productive activity during the summer months.
    d. All of the above

69. Plagiarism of materials is a common unethical practice by students. To help prevent it, a school librarian should do all of the following EXCEPT:
    a. Early in the school year, teach a lesson to students about the ethical use of materials, how to put information in their own words, and the possible penalties for plagiarism.
    b. Give teachers a list of websites that sell research papers.
    c. Purchase software such as Turnitin.com that checks for plagiarism.
    d. Notify the principal and send a letter to the student's parents whenever a student is observed using a website that sells research papers or copying material from the Internet into a report.

70. Which of the following actions taken by a librarian will best contribute to a library free of barriers?
    a. Make sure that library chairs are the appropriate size for age groups that use the library.
    b. Arrange books on shelves so that they can easily be reached from a wheelchair and are neither too high nor too close to the floor.
    c. Have an area with a couch set aside for students to sit comfortably and read.
    d. Automate the checkout process so it proceeds smoothly and students do not have to wait.

71. What is the educational impact of creating a comfortable reading area in the library, perhaps one with a couch or large armchair?
    a. This area makes the library seem more like home than an institution.
    b. The noise level in the library is reduced if some students are quietly reading.
    c. Students may be challenged to select more difficult, challenging books to read.
    d. Students will be encouraged to read when given a comfortable area, and their reading skills may increase with practice.

72. A librarian accesses some research models to help students find information for a report. Next, she shows students how to find these research models and tells them why they are more helpful than Google. What reasons does she give?
    a. The research models are not as commercial as Google is.
    b. Students can gain more detailed information from specific research models.
    c. Her school district recommends this research model.
    d. These research models are easier to use than search engines.

73. What kind of support may a librarian expect and seek from the Parents Organization at her school?
    a. The Parents Organization may collect and donate books to the school library.
    b. The Parents Organization may hold fundraising activities, such as a school carnival, to raise funds that are donated to the school library.
    c. The Parents Organization may find volunteers to help in the school library.
    d. All of the above

Copyright © Mometrix Media. You have been licensed one copy of this document for personal use only. Any other reproduction or redistribution is strictly prohibited. All rights reserved.

Question 74 pertains to the following conversation:

Librarian:	Juan, how can I help you today?
Juan:	I need something about World War II.
Librarian:	Are you going to write a report about World War II?
Juan:	Actually, no. We are going to have a debate.
Librarian:	About the whole war?
Juan:	No, just about the U.S. dropping that bomb on Hiroshima.
Librarian:	Which side will you take in the debate, Juan?
Juan:	I am on the side that will argue that the bombing was justified.

Librarian: I know just the materials you want. We have some books over here. One is the autobiography of a man who was on that bombing flight. Over there, we have some DVDs with films of the aftermath and also an interview with President Truman during which the president explains his reasoning for giving the order to drop the bomb. And I'll write a list of websites where you can find more information.

74. Which of the competencies for a beginning librarian did the librarian fulfill in this conversation?

    a. Effectively interviews patrons to determine information needs
    b. Applies bibliographic and retrieval techniques for organizing and using information sources
    c. Employs a variety of techniques to guide the development of independent readers
    d. Understands the role of the school library program as a central element in the intellectual life of the school

75. In a school with a fixed library schedule, a classroom teacher asks the librarian if she could bring her class for two consecutive periods next week instead of the usual one. She has assigned her students to work in teams on different aspects of the U.S. Revolutionary War and feels that they will need more than just one class period to complete this research. What realistic but helpful response may the librarian give?

    a. Regretfully tell the teacher she has no extra time in her schedule. The school is on a fixed schedule and there are no "free periods." Suggest that small groups come to library on their free time at recess and lunch period.
    b. Respond that the library will be overcrowded if everyone in the class is looking for materials simultaneously. Suggest that the students come in shifts to do their research, perhaps team by team.
    c. Juggle the schedule, trading one teacher's period for another if necessary, to allow for the one-time-only extra time period and offer to start the class off by teaching some Internet research techniques and showing students where relevant books are located in the library.
    d. Decline the double period request because of the fixed library schedule but offer to pull a cart of relevant books instead and deliver these to the classroom.

76. A librarian's school has just been granted funding to hire a media clerk. The principal has asked the librarian to draw up a job description for the new position. Which of these items is not part of an appropriate job description for a media clerk?

    a. Assists in the checking in and checking out of library materials
    b. Shelves materials as they are returned to the library
    c. Prepares monthly library reports
    d. Assists students who need help with research

Copyright © Mometrix Media. You have been licensed one copy of this document for personal use only. Any other reproduction or redistribution is strictly prohibited. All rights reserved.

77. A librarian is approached by a student who wants to do an Internet search for Thomas Jefferson but does not know how. The student has been assigned to read a biography of Jefferson and then write a report on his life, which is due in ten days. What is the librarian's best course of action in this situation?

  a. The librarian shows the student how to do an Internet search using Google.

  b. Since the assignment is to read a biography, the librarian directs the student to the biography section of the library rather than to the Internet. She helps the student select a biography at his reading level.

  c. The librarian directs the student to database that will quickly provide a list of resources and articles pertaining to Thomas Jefferson.

  d. The librarian searches her computerized records, decides that none of the biographies in her school library are appropriate for this student, and initiates an inter-library loan. The borrowed biography will take about two weeks to arrive.

78. Which of the following activities would best encourage students to become independent readers?

  a. A contest that awards a prize to students who read the most pages in a given time

  b. A student book club that meets weekly after school to discuss books they read

  c. A book fair at which students and parents can purchase books

  d. All of the above

79. Which of the following would not be a suitable organization for a librarian to join as part of her commitment to the library profession?

  a. The International Reading Association

  b. The Scott O'Dell Historical Fiction Organization

  c. The National Association of Librarians

  d. The Association for Technology in Education

80. In her media center, a librarian includes some audio CDs of books that are often assigned to students to read for their Language Arts class. She offers the recording along with the printed book to certain students. Which students should be allowed to use these audio books?

  a. Students who have hearing difficulties

  b. Any student who requests an audio version of a book

  c. Students who are struggling with reading skills

  d. Students who have an auditory learning style

81. Now that automated cataloging systems like MARC are available, when would a librarian need to use the Dewey Decimal system?

  a. When shelving books in the library

  b. When checking whether or not a book is checked out

  c. When preparing the monthly report for the library

  d. When helping a patron use the card catalogue

82. What is a computer network?

  a. A method for going online with a computer

  b. A group of interconnected computers

  c. A type of email used among employees or workers

  d. An advanced anti-viral safety device

Copyright © Mometrix Media. You have been licensed one copy of this document for personal use only. Any other reproduction or redistribution is strictly prohibited. All rights reserved.

83. When materials are carefully cataloged and processed, the most important result is that:
    a. The library looks neat and well organized.
    b. Students and staff can easily find books and other materials.
    c. The librarian can devote more time to helping students.
    d. The librarian will probably receive a good evaluation.

84. Which document should be signed by both parents and students before that student may use the school's library computers?
    a. Acceptable Use Policy
    b. Right to Information Act
    c. Federal Privacy Policy
    d. Copyright Law for Students and Teachers

85. A librarian asks teachers to inform her as far ahead of time as possible about research projects and other reading or literature-oriented activities they are planning. What is her primary reason for this request?
    a. She can set aside books on the topic reserved for a particular class.
    b. She can plan a research lesson keyed to the area of study.
    c. She can pull a cart of materials to be delivered to the teacher's classroom.
    d. All of the above

86. The library has received a large number of new acquisitions. How can the librarian best inform the staff about these new materials so that they can begin to use them?
    a. Make an announcement during the regular morning announcements and read aloud all the new titles.
    b. Circulate a memo advising staff members that new materials have arrived and asking that they check with the librarian to find out what they are.
    c. Post a list of the new materials on the checkout desk in the library.
    d. Announce at the next regular staff meeting that new materials have arrived, give a brief summary of what they are, and give teachers a handout that lists all the materials.

87. A middle school librarian is drawing up a budget to present to the principal for future funding of the library. She wants to shift library use from fixed scheduling to flexible scheduling and realizes this will require additional funding. What is a reasonable length of time for the librarian to forecast the completion of the shift so that the additional expenses can be gradually phased in?
    a. Sometime during the next school year, a period of nine months
    b. One year
    c. Two to four years
    d. Three to five years

88. Which of the following activities would be best to have as part of a "family night at the library"?
    a. Story time for young children
    b. Book reviews of favorite books given by students who have read these books
    c. A talk by the librarian on how the library functions
    d. A speech by the principal on future goals for the library

Copyright © Mometrix Media. You have been licensed one copy of this document for personal use only.
Any other reproduction or redistribution is strictly prohibited. All rights reserved.

89. A librarian has arranged for a well-known historian to speak at the library on the topics of why history excites him and the methods he uses for research, both on the Internet and in books. Which of the following would be the best way to make sure that the community is aware of this event and invited to attend it?

    a. The librarian arranges for an announcement of the date and time of this event to be made during the school's morning announcements.

    b. The librarian draws up a flyer and sends copies to each classroom for students to take home.

    c. The librarian informs the local television station and invites them to send a film crew. She asks that a mention of the event be made during the evening news a few days before.

    d. As she meets with her scheduled daily classes, the librarian tells each class about the event and asks them to invite their families.

90. A student is using a library computer to research information about World War II. Among the websites she locates is one that represents a neo-Nazi group. How can the librarian help the student determine whether information from this website is factual and unbiased?

    a. The librarian can tell the student that this website is biased and not to trust it.

    b. The librarian can assist the student in finding information on the same topic from a different viewpoint. This situation provides the librarian with an opportunity to teach the student how to assess the reliability of information found on the Internet.

    c. The librarian can make sure that the library's filter will block that website in the future.

    d. The librarian can suggest that the student find three or four more resources before making a decision about this one.

91. A good way for a school librarian to assess students' performance is to:

    a. Start each lesson with a pop quiz on the last lesson.

    b. Point out student errors during discussion so that they will not repeat them.

    c. Incorporate unacceptable behavior into the grades she gives.

    d. Enlist the help of students in creating an evaluation system so that they understand and have some ownership of it.

92. Why is it important for a school librarian to be able to demonstrate that her media center helps students meet national and state standards?

    a. Education today is standards-based.

    b. Meeting standards will cause the principal to look favorably on budget requests.

    c. Standards help organize the content of instruction.

    d. All of the above

93. When a librarian is arranging the media center, an important consideration in the placement of the computer lab should be:

    a. Indirect lighting so that computer screens will be easily visible to students

    b. The arrangement of computers so that each one can be seen by the librarian

    c. The age and possible malfunctions of the computers

    d. The placement of computers in a quiet part of the library so that students will not be distracted

Copyright © Mometrix Media. You have been licensed one copy of this document for personal use only. Any other reproduction or redistribution is strictly prohibited. All rights reserved.

94. The circulation policy of a school media center needs to be fair and somewhat flexible because:
    a. Students cannot always pay fines for overdue books.
    b. Automated circulation procedures are easier to misuse.
    c. The circulation policy controls the ease of access to materials in the media center.
    d. Different materials should have different checkout periods.

95. Last week, a librarian taught students how to access certain databases. This week, the students are given the assignment to locate one database and answer questions based on what they find there. As the librarian moves from computer to computer, she observes that only a few of the students are managing to access the assigned database and, once there, are having trouble obtaining the answers to the assigned questions. What is the librarian's best course of action?
    a. Help students individually at their computers.
    b. End this unsuccessful assignment and use the period for student reading time.
    c. Have the students leave their computers and gather around the librarian so that she can provide them with oral instructions about what to do.
    d. Have the students leave their computers and gather around one computer so that they can observe the librarian as she models what they should do.

96. A librarian is helping a student create a Power Point presentation that he is going to give to his classmates and teachers. Which of the following concepts should the librarian bring to the student's attention as he creates his Power Point presentation?
    a. Design
    b. Content
    c. Audience
    d. All of the above

97. What is the most important reason for a librarian to spend all her library funds before the administration "sweeps" the school's accounts?
    a. A sweep means that remaining library funds will become unavailable.
    b. A sweep before funds are spent will reduce the next year's funding.
    c. The school expects her to use her budget every year.
    d. The administration will be unhappy if she is seen as postponing expenditures.

98. The main focus of the lessons a librarian presents to classes should be:
    a. How to use the Dewey Decimal System
    b. Information literacy concepts
    c. Improving students' reading skills
    d. Exposing students to literature at the appropriate grade level

99. When is using interlibrary loan a better idea than purchasing the book or material?
    a. When the book is too expensive
    b. When the book is controversial
    c. When the book is about an obscure subject
    d. When the book has been out of print for over five years

Copyright © Mometrix Media. You have been licensed one copy of this document for personal use only. Any other reproduction or redistribution is strictly prohibited. All rights reserved.

100. What is the primary advantage of networking with librarians in other schools?
   a. A librarian will acquire advocates who will support her when she proposes a new idea for her library.
   b. A librarian will receive information about other libraries that she can use to improve her own program.
   c. A librarian will have a group of friends who have their work in common.
   d. A librarian will educate other librarians on new methods and technologies.

Copyright © Mometrix Media. You have been licensed one copy of this document for personal use only. Any other reproduction or redistribution is strictly prohibited. All rights reserved.

Answer Key and Explanations

1. B: Call the parents and ask them to help the student return the book.
Parents will often know where the book is, will remind the child to return it, or will know if the book is lost or destroyed. Answer A would violate student privacy rules and embarrass the student. Answer C is incorrect because the responsibility of dealing with an overdue book lies with the librarian, not the principal. Answer D is incorrect because the librarian does not yet know if the book has been lost or destroyed.

2. C: Check with the principal to be sure of the school calendar and any school or district guidelines for fundraising activities.
The school or district may have guidelines for fundraising activities. Discussing the book fair first with the principal is a collegial action, should help gain his/her support for the project, and clears the school calendar for the book fair date(s). Answers A, B and D are all appropriate activities, but they should take place after discussing the proposed book fair and its date with the principal.

3. D: Move the collection to higher shelves.
Lower shelves do not allow wheelchair or handicapped access. Answers A and B are good ideas for non-handicapped students, but librarians are required to maintain a "barrier free" library environment. Answer C is incorrect because it does not address the problem of the books' location.

4. D: American Union of Library Employees.
There is no such organization as the American Union of Library Employees. The other three answer choices are well-known professional associations that librarians should be encouraged to join in order to take advantage of their resources and support.

5. A: The book contains material that is outdated or inaccurate.
As time passes, new information may supplant older, less accurate information. Books that will give the reader inaccurate information should be removed from the collection. Answers B and D are incorrect because organizations or parents should not make decisions about what books belong in the library. In conjunction with school and district administrators, the librarian will follow the district selection policy to determine the appropriateness of books in the collection. Answer C is incorrect because frequency of use should not govern when a book should be discarded. That rarely-used book may be the exact one needed by a student doing special research.

6. D: All of the above.
Each of the given actions will help make the change to a flexible schedule more acceptable to administrators and staff members.

Copyright © Mometrix Media. You have been licensed one copy of this document for personal use only.
Any other reproduction or redistribution is strictly prohibited. All rights reserved.

7. B: When cataloging new books for the library collection.
The MARC system is an electronic program for cataloging books. It replaces old card catalogs with a more efficient and user-friendly form of storing information.
A is incorrect because weeding involves subtracting books from the collection, not adding them. The MARC system would not know if a book is damaged or its content outdated. C is incorrect because arranging books on the shelves is a physical action that involves a number of factors not tracked by the MARC system. D is incorrect because the MARC system is not a spreadsheet and is not designed for budgetary use.

8. A: Yes, under the Fair Usage provision of the copyright law.
The Fair Usage provision of the copyright law states that copying and using selected parts of copyrighted works for specific educational purposes is permitted, especially if the copies are made spontaneously and are used temporarily. B is incorrect because of the Fair Usage provisions stated above. C is incorrect because the principal is not the person who can grant permission to use copyrighted materials. D is incorrect because copying just one page and using it temporarily does not cause any loss of income to the author.

9. B: Create a display of books and other materials on ethnic topics and invite students and parents to visit one evening and browse the display. Then, have a discussion period during which parents and children are invited to share special aspects of their heritages and customs.
This is the best activity because it involves both the community students in celebrating diversity. A might embarrass some students. C might involve spending a large part of the budget on books that only a few students would use. D might embarrass students because they are asked to speak in a language they may be just learning without any prior preparation.

10. C: After conferring with each classroom teacher about his or her current curriculum, demonstrate separately to different classes how to use the Internet to find information on the topic each class is presently studying.
Teaching different classes to find materials they can use best supports the specific projects of each class. Students are more likely to pay attention to a demonstration if it involves something they need to do.
A is incorrect because it leaves students on their own to blunder around trying to use an unfamiliar process. B is a good idea, but it takes the "one size fits all" approach to instruction. D is not the best approach because it encourages students to figure out a process by themselves, without teacher instruction or help.

11. C: Obtain the book through interlibrary loan.
By using interlibrary loan, a librarian can expand access to books without exceeding the school's library budget. Answer A is not the best choice; since the book is not already in the school collection, it is probably one that not many students or teachers would use. Because of interlibrary loan, the librarian does not have to spend funds that may be needed for something else. B is not a good choice because the alternate resource may not be exactly what the teacher needs. In many cases, the teacher has already done some research to determine that a particular book is the one that best meets her needs. Answer D hands the problem over to another library and requires the teacher to make a visit that may or may not be successful.

Copyright © Mometrix Media. You have been licensed one copy of this document for personal use only.
Any other reproduction or redistribution is strictly prohibited. All rights reserved.

12. D: Soliciting paid advertising to run on the library's website.
If the library's website runs advertising promoting community bookstores, restaurants, or other local businesses that pay for this advertising, a conflict of interest might result. A, B, and C are common practices and are generally successful ways to raise funds.

13. C: Research all applicable national, state, and district standards.
The librarian should thoroughly read all applicable standards and write a statement that complies with them. Answer A is incorrect because the principal may not be familiar with all the standards that apply to school libraries. Answer B is incorrect because other districts may have different standards from the ones that apply to this particular school library. Answer D is incorrect because the librarian does not need the superintendent's permission to draw up a statement of library standards; oftentimes, the superintendent or principal has asked the librarian to do this.

14. C: Demonstrate to the class how to use the library's computers for research.
Answer A might involve leaving the library unsupervised and also may be viewed by the teacher as intrusive. Answers B and D are good ideas, but students who do not know how to use the library's computers for research will benefit most from demonstration and instruction.

15. A: Hold a brief staff meeting to instruct teachers and library staff in using the new software. If the staff knows how to use the software, they can assist individual students right away, even before students receive instruction from the librarian during their next scheduled library visit. Also, staff members should become familiar with all new technology. Choice B risks that not all teachers will read the memo and be able to help their students use the software. C is the second action the librarian should take, but since she cannot meet with every class in one day, informing the teachers first is more important. D would carry individualized instruction to an extreme. The librarian would be unable to perform other tasks if she attempted to show students one at a time how to use the software.

16. C: Ask the student if he or she would like some help and abide by the student's response.
Some students would prefer to discover things by themselves without adult intervention. Answer A would result in success this time, but the student would not learn how to locate information in the future. Answer B involves waiting too long; frustrated students are not good learners. D is a good idea, but it should only be done if the student consents. Step C should come before D.

17. A: *The Horn Book.*
This journal specializes in reviewing books at the elementary level. Answers B and C are incorrect because these resources mainly review adult literature. Answer D is incorrect because only books in the field of mathematics are discussed in the *MAA Reviews.*

18. C: Monitoring student use of cell phones.
Student cell phone use is not part of the librarian's technological skill areas. The responsibility for students who bring cell phones to school belongs to the school, if it has regulations regarding cell phones at school, and if not, to the classroom teacher. Responsibilities described in Answers A, B, and D are increasingly becoming part of the school librarian's job description.

Copyright © Mometrix Media. You have been licensed one copy of this document for personal use only. Any other reproduction or redistribution is strictly prohibited. All rights reserved.

19. C: Consider ways to make the report more meaningful and design a new format.
The beginning librarian is better off not making any radical changes early in the term, especially if there is a required format for the monthly report. In the beginning, the report should look similar to the one from last year. The principal will expect and understand this format. Changes in it can be made gradually throughout the school year. Answers A, B and D are all good ways to prepare for writing the monthly report.

20. D: All of the above.
Each of the above statistics adds to the significance of a librarian's monthly report.

21. B: Collaborative projects with teachers.
The primary purpose of the monthly report is to inform the principal how productive the library has been. This productivity includes more than circulation statistics. It includes projects the librarian has worked on with classroom teachers. Answer A is not a good choice because interpersonal problems, or infractions of the rules, are best dealt with informally and verbally. If written down, they may start conflicts or inflate concerns. Answer C is something to include in an annual budget request. A report details past events, not future plans. The same reasoning applies in Answer D. The monthly library report is not the proper venue for budget requests, although it is possible to write the report in such a way that it hints at future needs.

22. B: The card catalog.
OPAC is a computerized catalog that patrons can use to search for resources. Answer A, The MARC system is a data base that can be accessed through OPAC. Answer C, The Dewey Decimal system is a system for manually organizing library materials based on common subject matter, and is still used for shelving books in the library and locating books. The Reader's Guide to Periodical Literature is a printed guide to locating periodic materials. It is being replaced by similar online services.

23. B: The visit will contribute to literature appreciation for all students.
The exposure to a successful writer will encourage students in their own writing, as well as encourage them to read the writer's books. Answer A is incorrect because while media attention may be a positive result of the visit, it is not the main reason. Library-generated activities should be focused on what is best for students. Answer C is incorrect for the same reason. The library might increase its funds a little, but that would not be the main, student-centered reason for inviting the author. Answer D is also a good result, but adding to statistics would not be the purpose for the visit.

24. B: Have students work on the assignment in pairs or small groups. Assign students to groups in which each struggling ESL student will have a partner to help him or her understand and complete the assignment. Encourage groups or pairs to ask for help as needed.
Peer-based instruction is more likely to be accepted by an ESL student and is less embarrassing than if the student were singled out by the librarian for individual help. Answer A singles out these students and, in fact, leaves them out. The librarian may not have time for individual instruction later on. Meanwhile, the class will have moved beyond these students in computer research skills. Answer C does not guarantee that the ESL students will understand the instructions, even if they are given slowly and in simple language. These students may not ask for help because of not wanting to be singled out for their language difficulties. Some may simply not attempt the assignment. Answer D also does not guarantee understanding. Students who do not have enough English vocabulary will probably not understand written instructions better than oral ones.

Copyright © Mometrix Media. You have been licensed one copy of this document for personal use only. Any other reproduction or redistribution is strictly prohibited. All rights reserved.

25. B: Quietly discuss with the student the rules about plagiarism, show him ways to put information in his own words, and ask to see his report when he has rewritten it.
By handling the matter in a firm but low-key way, the librarian will avoid embarrassing the student or making him defensive. However, to make sure he understood her explanation of plagiarism, the librarian should ask to see his report after he writes it in his own words. Answer A, notifying the teacher, passes on the problem to someone else. The teacher has not observed what the librarian has observed; therefore, the problem is best handled by the librarian. Answer C also passes on the problem and inflates it as well. It is possible the student did not understand about plagiarism. He should be given a second chance. Answer D also assumes that the student should be treated as a habitual offender. It might be a good choice should he plagiarize a second time.

26. A: Weeding and schedule changing.
Librarians need to know the library's content thoroughly before deciding what materials to weed and what to acquire. If a librarian discards a teacher's favorite materials, she will lose a supporter of the library. The librarian should wait awhile before weeding. Answer B should be done early in the year so that staff members understand that plagiarism is widespread, sometimes inadvertent, and what teachers can do about it. Answer C is always a good idea whenever the librarian can find time in the school and library schedule. Answer D, reorganizing the furniture, can be done right away. The arrangement of the librarian's space should reflect her personal philosophy and competency.

27. D: Hearing stories read aloud contributes to students' interest in reading.
Answer A is one reason why story hours are sometimes scheduled, but it is not an educational, student-centered reason. Answer B may be a result of a story hour, but it is not the main reason for this activity. Answer C may happen incidentally, but reading instruction itself is the responsibility of the classroom teacher.

28. A: Knowing about changes to the curriculum and participating in making those changes will enable the librarian to acquire materials that support the new curriculum.
Answer B is not correct because the planned curriculum committee is at the district level. Answer C is not likely. Librarians and teachers are all given documents explaining state curriculum requirements. Answer D is also unlikely.

29. A: Instructing them in effective ways to do research on the Internet and in efficient use of library reference materials and books on the library shelves.
Answer A fulfills both the librarian's responsibilities and the students' needs. Instruction of this sort can be tailored to ongoing classroom projects and individualized to meet the needs of students who need support, as well as students who can work on their own. Answer B does not produce any educational results. Part of assigned library time should be set aside for exchanging books, but not all of it. Answer C is like a "story time" for older students, although making students aware of new materials should be part of the librarian's instructional plans from time to time. Although answer D is very helpful to the librarian, it is of little educational value to the students.

30. D: All of the above.
By determining teachers' needs in advance, the librarian can give maximum assistance at the proper time and integrate the teacher's curriculum into her own.

Copyright © Mometrix Media. You have been licensed one copy of this document for personal use only. Any other reproduction or redistribution is strictly prohibited. All rights reserved.

31. C: Organizing space into areas that can be flexibly arranged to accommodate different sizes of groups as well as community activities held after school.
Answer A is probably not feasible in a library where the walls are filled with student work and other materials. The furniture size is probably already fixed in this library, and although it should accommodate students of different sizes, this is not a factor of room arrangement. Answer D is probably not feasible either, given that most libraries have bookshelves and small corners that cannot all be observed from the desk. Even if D could be accomplished, it still would not be most important aspect of arranging the library.

32. C: Student-produced work.

33. B: Have an open house in the library once a month and invite families to browse the library's collection and get to know the librarian.
Answer A is too restrictive, involving only some students. Answer C is also too limited, involving only the option of research and, again, only students. Answer D assumes that all parents can receive e-mail, which may not be true. Also, the scheduled hours might not work for certain families.

34. A: Using a variety of instructional techniques that actively involve students in listening, working with various media and materials, reading, and writing.
Answer B is not really feasible in a library setting. It would involve the librarian rushing from group to group and being unable to supervise the groups. Answer C would have the same problem, besides possibly embarrassing slower learners. Answer D is incorrect because a correct solution is offered.

35. D: The librarian should use electronic and print media to inform families and communities.

36. C: An Acceptable Use Policy.
An acceptable use policy outlines allowable Internet access. In order to access school computers, parents and students usually must agree to this policy in writing. On occasion, filters on library computer block a whole category, parts of which may contain information useful to students. The librarian should be able to unblock some harmless sites for specific reasons. Answer A is incorrect because the Patriot Act affects libraries mainly by attempting to seek lists of materials borrowed by certain users. Answer B, the No Child Left Behind Act, refers to academic progress and school accountability, not to acceptable Internet use. MARC records are used to track library materials and their usage.

37. B: Using keywords with "or," "but," or "and."
A Boolean search enables a researcher to define precise limits for searches. For example, a student might enter "temples *and* Greece *but* not Athens" if looking for Greek temples that are not in Athens. Answer A is incorrect because mathematics is not involved in a Boolean search, although a certain level of logic is required. Answer C is incorrect because a Boolean search does not require a special database. Answer D is incorrect because the Dewey Decimal System is a way of organizing information, not a way of searching the Internet.

Copyright © Mometrix Media. You have been licensed one copy of this document for personal use only. Any other reproduction or redistribution is strictly prohibited. All rights reserved.

38. D: Critiquing books.
The librarian should remain neutral about books and other materials in the library's collection, recognizing that there are many points of view on an issue and many writing styles. The librarian is responsible for scheduling classes and library-related events, reporting on the functioning and collection of the library, and maintaining and facilitating circulation of the library's materials.

39. C: Speak to the boys firmly about proper library behavior.
Since the students are in the library, they are on the librarian's territory, and she has as much responsibility as the teacher to see that they behave correctly. The teacher has had a chance to correct these boys but has not done it. Speaking to him about their behavior might embarrass the teacher or make him resentful. He might continue to ignore it. After it is clear that the teacher is aware of the behavior and is choosing not to intervene, the librarian should corral the unruly students and remind them how to behave in the library. Answer D is not necessary because the problem can be handled by the librarian without the need to hand it over to someone else.

40. B: Draw up a complete job description of the position
Before a media clerk can be hired, the librarian must have a clear plan for how best to use this person's skills. Also, the applicant needs to know exactly what the job entails. The librarian should draw up the job description and then search for someone to fill it. The job description can also serve as the basis for evaluating the media clerk later on. Answer A would be a good second step. Answer C is not a good idea because it limits the pool of applicants to those the librarian already knows. Answer D is not a very productive idea because each library is unique and has its own needs.

41. C: Form a committee of interested teachers to help weed the collection at a time that is convenient for everyone. If teachers are involved in the process of weeding, they will support the idea and be content with its results. The librarian should seek faculty help for this task. Answer A, canceling classes, would deprive some students of instruction and book selection opportunities and might be in violation of the librarian's contract. Answer B is feasible but puts the entire decision-making task on the shoulders of the librarian. Also, it calls for working extra hours. Answer D is not a good idea because students do not yet have a clear grasp of criteria for keeping or removing a book from the library collection.

42. D: All of the above.
The librarian is responsible for encouraging students to become independent readers. There are several strategies that help accomplish this goal, including the three listed above.

43. A: Ask the student what his assignment is and what kind of books he is looking for.
Before the librarian can effectively help the student, she must interview him about his needs. If his answer is vague, such as, "Well, I have to write this science paper," she should ask him a series of questions until she understands his exact need. Then, she can assist him in finding appropriate materials. Answer B assumes that the student knows what book he wants and does not know how to find it. This may not be the case. He may not know what book will help him. Answer C puts the problem off until another time, and the student may have a deadline to complete his assignment. Answer D takes valuable library time away from the student assigned help, and that student will not know as much as the librarian does about available materials.

Copyright © Mometrix Media. You have been licensed one copy of this document for personal use only. Any other reproduction or redistribution is strictly prohibited. All rights reserved.

44. C: Use OPAC to find MARC entries about Monarch butterfly migration.
The student clearly needs guidance in locating research materials. OPAC is a computerized catalog that will help narrow his search to appropriate materials. The Dewey Decimal System has been replaced in most libraries with computerized catalogs like OPAC. B might be a helpful suggestion, but the topic is so broad that too many responses would probably be generated. D, the *Readers' Guide to Periodical Literature*, is another outdated print resource now generally replaced by online data resources.

45. C: Send a note home with students inviting parents to a "parents' night" at the library.
Sending a note home with students is often an unreliable way to communicate. Not all students remember to take home a note, or if they do take it home, many forget to give it to parents. Using the school newsletter and/or school website will be more effective. In your message asking for volunteers, remember to make volunteering in the library sound as interesting as it really is. For parents' night, serve refreshments, display students' work, and consider having a few students talk to the group about how they use the library.

46. C: Make a comprehensive daily, weekly, and monthly plan listing what needs to be done, the deadline for completing each task, and the person responsible for handling the task.
Making a detailed plan of goals, needs, assigned times, etc. will clearly lay out for the librarian what her tasks are. She can estimate the time required for each and assign a date and time for completion of each item. Answer A would not be the best first step, because after making the plan, it may be evident that the media clerk is already performing all that he/she can handle. Answer B might be a good second step, but it is not a good first step. If the library has traditionally managed with the number of employees it presently has, then the problem is more likely to be time management than the need for more help. After the beginning librarian has made her plans, she can show the principal item by item what the problems are and ask for his help if it turns out that her workload is indeed excessive. Answer D, putting in overtime hours, may be necessary but that fact will not be clear until the planning takes place. An exhausted librarian will not be efficient, so that option is not the most desirable.

47. B: Discuss her plans for change with the principal and get his/her input about the concept and affordability of flexible scheduling, as well as the potential costs to the library of hosting special events.
There is likely to be a financial component to making these changes. In some school settings, having a flexible schedule means that the school must hire someone to give the teachers the prep periods they formerly had during a fixed schedule. Hosting special events can require extended hours for a school's custodial staff, along with additional electrical and heating expenses. The librarian needs to find out from the principal if the school budget can handle these changes. Also, as a matter of diplomacy, obtaining the principal's support for a change in practice is a good management technique. Answer A could cause dissension among staff members and bring criticism from an uninformed principal. Answer C is the easy way out, but it will not result in achievement of the librarian's goals. Answer D is a good second step for the librarian to take after she has obtained the support of the principal.

Copyright © Mometrix Media. You have been licensed one copy of this document for personal use only. Any other reproduction or redistribution is strictly prohibited. All rights reserved.

48. D: All of the above.
The librarian's vision for her media center should be written in a goal statement, perhaps with a reasonable time frame included if expensive changes are foreseen. After drawing up the statement (A), the librarian should share it with the principal (B), and get that person's feedback and suggestions, which can be included in a new draft of the goal statement to be shared with school district administration or the school board (C). This way, the librarian will find out if all of her goals are considered feasible and important by the people who will fund most of them.

49. B: Hardware is a physical component of a computer, such as a monitor, RAM, CPU, hard drive, or motherboard. Software is a series of coded instructions that direct the computer to perform certain operations.
Hardware includes the physical parts of a computer that a person can touch. Software consists of the programs that run the hardware, such as a browser, operating system, or word processing program. Answers A, C and D all refer to software items on a computer.

50. B: A telephone call to each family.
A telephone call to each family would require too much time, when it is possible to speak with a number of families at the same time through teleconferencing. A Power Point presentation to the parents club or school board or a community organization can be a very effective way to demonstrate the library in action during the school day. A newsletter will inform parents of what is going on in the media center and of future dates for upcoming events, such as a parents' night, after-school book club, or book fair.

51. A: The librarian should accept the invitation because business people can support the media center in several ways, including donating computers, giving money for library projects, and supporting the goals and visions of the librarian and her school. By attending the luncheon, she will create good will for the school and the library.
Answer B is incorrect in stating that making connections with the business community is not part of the librarian's job. This responsibility is specifically mentioned in Domain II, Competency 004. Also, creating good will in the community is important in order to have community support of the school and the library. Answer C offers a negative view of this opportunity. Through her speech and her handout, the librarian can impact the business community present at the meeting and the wider business community consisting of the members' friends and associates. She can explain the rationale behind the operation of a modern media center. There is no reason to think that her audience will not pay attention. Answer D also offers a negative view of the reason for her invitation. After the librarian's speech, there will probably be a question and answer period during which she can clear up any misconceptions.

52. B: You may exchange information from each other's databases.
Answer A is incorrect because interlibrary loan is an easier way to obtain books students need that are not in your library. Answer C may be true, but that fact does not help the librarian in her job. Answer D is incorrect because once a librarian discovers what is in the collections of these libraries, she can use interlibrary loan to obtain needed materials on a temporary basis without having to purchase the books.

Copyright © Mometrix Media. You have been licensed one copy of this document for personal use only.
Any other reproduction or redistribution is strictly prohibited. All rights reserved.

53. D: Check the items received against the purchase orders.
As items arrive, it is important to first make sure that everything ordered in each purchase order has been received in the library. Answer A is incorrect because books will probably be processed with spine labels before they are shipped. Answers B and C are necessary actions to take after checking off the arriving items.

54. B: To verify that the subject matter is accurate and covers student and teacher needs.
Through this review, the librarian may discover that some subjects are not properly covered in the database, and she may need to purchase others. Answer A is incorrect because a review of the database will not reveal student plagiarism. Answer C is incorrect because a filter prevents students from accessing inappropriate sites. This information is not found on a database. Answer D is incorrect because students with a variety of reading skills will access each database.

55. D: Bibliography.
A bibliography is not usually a part of a visual presentation such as Power Point. The purpose of a Power Point presentation is to engage the audience visually. Techniques for doing this would be the main points of a lesson in creating Power Point presentations. A bibliography might be in the form of a handout to the audience after the presentation.

56. B: Raise money for library needs and projects.
A visit by a writer is not likely to bring in much, if any, money for the library. If copies of the writer's books are sold to students so that he can autograph them, he will probably supply those copies and receive the funds from the sales. The purpose of having a visiting writer is expressed in the other three choices. The visit will encourage student interest in reading and writing, which may be evidenced by an increase in circulation. Some students may develop an interest in reading or writing they did not previously have, with the possible goal of becoming a writer themselves.

57. D: Integrating technology into the library program
By creating an interesting activity that prompts students to discover the functions of various computer programs, the librarian is integrating computer technology into the library program. Answer A, ethical use, does not apply here, as nothing is copied or plagiarized during the search. Answer B also does not apply because diversity is not an issue. Everyone is equal when using a computer. Answer C does not apply because the students are not using oral or written communication.

58. C: She should accept the opportunity but make phone calls to voters and give television interviews on her own time.
It is very likely that the librarian's school district will appreciate her involvement in promoting the measure. Public school employees are usually prohibited from political involvement in the classroom or during the school day but not necessarily on their own time. Answer B is exactly the opposite of what the librarian should do. She should not advocate a funding measure in the library or give students handouts about it. Answer D is something she can do casually, during conversations in the staff room, but she is also free to promote the legislation more than that on her own time. In fact, according to Domain III, she should do so.

Copyright © Mometrix Media. You have been licensed one copy of this document for personal use only. Any other reproduction or redistribution is strictly prohibited. All rights reserved.

59. B: The length of time any one student may be allowed to spend on the Internet.
Student needs for Internet access vary by school, by program, and by the number of computers available for student use. The time constraints for usage should be determined school by school rather than through a district-wide Fair Use Policy. Answers A, C, and D should all be included in a district-wide Fair Use Policy.

60. A: Ask the teacher to give students the assignment and then schedule a time to bring the class to the library. Directly teach students research techniques for print materials and for the Internet. Show them how to locate internet databases that will meet their needs and how to coordinate information from several sources.
Answer A provides the best way for students to learn research techniques, especially since they will be interested because of the assignment. Answer B puts the entire burden on the teacher with no real assistance from the librarian. Answer C may not be possible unless the library has a media clerk who can be present if the librarian leaves the library. Also, it is really not necessary because the teacher can bring the class to the library. Answer D is also incorrect because another one of the answer choices is more appropriate.

61. B: Obtain a list of suspect databases from the concerned teacher and evaluate each one carefully to see if the information is accurate, reliable and unbiased. Remove these sources from the library's collection.
The librarian is the person responsible for assessing information from databases for accuracy and/or bias. Answer A, asking busy teachers to help with the problem, is asking them to do something they may not know how to do or have time to do. Answer C also puts the burden on the teacher when the responsibility for determining accuracy is the librarian's. Answer D is a good follow-up after the librarian has assessed the databases, but it is not the first step to take.

62. B: Since Power Point is a visual medium, she should take advantage of that and show what to do rather than lecturing about it. She can invite students to try some of the techniques she is teaching and make the lesson as hands-on as possible so that its content will cross the language barrier.
All students enjoy a hands-on lesson, and by giving one, the librarian is making sure that ESL students are not derided or embarrassed by their language difficulties. Answer A singles them out and excludes them from learning something they would benefit from knowing. Answer C is not feasible because the partner would not be understood any more than the librarian. Answer D is apt to embarrass ESL students, although speaking slowly and clearly is a good idea.

63. C: Use teleconferencing so that they all can exchange information at the same time.
Answer A, calling each volunteer, is a time-consuming way to meet with volunteers and also deprives them of the opportunity to interchange ideas. Answer B, composing an email response, may be a difficult task for some volunteers—not everyone is Internet savvy. Answer D requires volunteers to travel to school at a time that may not be convenient for them.

64. D: All of the above.
OPAC (Online Public Access Catalog) is an automated system that helps patrons search for library materials, tracks checked-out materials, and assists in purchasing and cataloging.

Copyright © Mometrix Media. You have been licensed one copy of this document for personal use only.
Any other reproduction or redistribution is strictly prohibited. All rights reserved.

65. D: The librarian should say that she will be happy to help organize a display of students' geography projects. After all, they did their geography research in the library. Other students will be inspired when they see the results of classroom work and library research.
School libraries should be decorated with student work. As for Answer A, the subject matter of the proposed display is not relevant. Libraries should contain material on all subjects. Answer B is a selfish response, actually indicating that the librarian finds changing the displays to be too much work. Answer C offers an unlikely possibility.

66. B: Written, in the form of a letter to the group.
A written response is best because it is a record of the school's decision in the matter. It can be used as evidence if the situation escalates and there are more protests. A, a phone call, would not be the best choice because there is no written record of what is said by both parties during the phone call. An e-mail is a form of written response but does not constitute evidence. Answer D might be seen as insulting by the group because there is no actual response to their complaint.

67. C: Evaluate the current collection and note any areas that lack materials.
Before the librarian can plan for the future, she must assess the present status of the school library's collection. If there are materials lacking that teachers have requested, these should have priority in the new collection. Answers A, B, and D are steps that need to be taken in the acquisition process, but evaluating what is on hand must be the first step.

68. D: All of the above.
Not all school librarians will have funds to do this, but giving students a book for the summer will help them keep up both their reading skills and their interest in reading, as well as engage them in a productive activity instead of just playing all summer.

69. D: Notify the principal and send a letter to the parents whenever a student is observed using a website that sells research papers or copying material from the Internet directly into her report.
Actions A, B and C will be helpful to teachers and students in the effort to prevent plagiarism. As for D, those actions should probably not be taken by the librarian. The librarian who observes a student in the library plagiarizing should speak to the student and perhaps to the teacher. Taking the matter farther, to the principal or the family, should be the teacher's responsibility. The teacher will know the student better than the librarian and will be aware if this attempt to plagiarize is a first effort or an ongoing problem.

70. B: Arrange books on shelves so that they can easily be reached from a wheelchair and are neither too high nor too close to the floor.
Having a barrier-free library means that the facilities are accessible to the handicapped. Answer A refers to having small chairs for young children and larger chairs for older children, a plan that is necessary but unrelated to having a barrier-free library. Answers C and D encourage all students to read but do not particularly accommodate handicapped students.

71. D: Students will be encouraged to read when given a comfortable area, and their reading skills may increase with practice.
A well-designed school library should include some space for private reading. If such space is available, students will be encouraged to read as a leisure-time activity and at the same time may increase their reading skills. Answer A is not an educational impact of a having reading area. Answer B does not refer to any benefits the student may derive.

Copyright © Mometrix Media. You have been licensed one copy of this document for personal use only. Any other reproduction or redistribution is strictly prohibited. All rights reserved.

72. B: Students can gain more detailed information from specific research models.
If school districts recommend or require the use of a specific research model, teachers and students will have the same framework for evaluating student projects. Answer A is not relevant because the financial backing of a particular research model does not reflect its relevance or the significance of its information. Answer C does not restrict the librarian to district-recommended materials. Answer D may or may not be true, but the importance of the task lies in the results, what students can find out by using these research models.

73. D: All of the above.
The school librarian should seek a relationship with the parents' organization at the school, because this organization is a source of funding, book donations, and volunteers.

74. A: Effectively interviews patrons to determine information needs.
Note that in the beginning of the conversation between Juan and the librarian, he is at first vague and general about his topic. The librarian asks a series of skillful questions to narrow down the subject area and is then able to help Juan. Answer B would apply to the librarian's knowledge of appropriate materials, but her primary action in the conversation is to determine Juan's information needs. Answer C is incorrect because Juan is not trying to improve his reading skills. He is looking for information. Answer D deals with the librarian's philosophy and not with her ability to discover a patron's needs.

75. C: Juggle the schedule, trading one teacher's period for another if necessary to allow for the one-time-only extra time period and offer to start the class off by teaching some Internet research techniques and showing students where relevant books are located in the library.
Even on a fixed schedule, there are a few free periods for students to come to the library and exchange books. The librarian could trade periods with another teacher (with that teacher's permission) who is normally scheduled for the period before or after one of those free periods. Prior to the scheduled time period, the librarian and teacher can discuss and plan relevant instruction in research skills for this class. Answer A is too inflexible and discounts the possibility of juggling schedules. Answer B is unlikely, because a whole class at a time is usually in the library, especially if the schedule is fixed. Answer C offers to provide some help to the teacher, but not as much as in answer C.

76. C: Prepares monthly library reports.
The preparation of monthly reports is the responsibility of the librarian. Checking in materials and shelving them, as well as helping students locate what they need, are part of the media clerk's job description.

77. B: Since the assignment is to read a biography, the librarian directs the student to the biography section of the library rather than to the Internet. She helps the student select a biography at his reading level.
In this particular case, the student will benefit more from using the library's own resources than from using the Internet. The school library will probably have a biography of Thomas Jefferson, and the arrival date for the interlibrary loan would be too late for the student's needs.

78. D: All of the above.
Each of these activities will encourage students to read.

Copyright © Mometrix Media. You have been licensed one copy of this document for personal use only. Any other reproduction or redistribution is strictly prohibited. All rights reserved.

79. B: Scott O'Dell Historical Fiction Organization.
The Scott O'Dell Organization awards an annual prize to an author of children's historical fiction. It is not a professional library organization. The other three are.

80. C: Students who are struggling with reading skills.
Some students who are having difficulty learning to read will benefit from "reading along" with a recording. They view and hear the words at the same time, which helps increase their reading vocabulary. Answer A describes students who would not benefit from listening to a story because they are hearing-impaired. Answer B is probably not a good idea because some students, even good readers, would be tempted to listen to the tape instead of reading the book. Answer D is incorrect because reading requires a visual mode, and learning style is irrelevant in this situation.

81. A: When shelving books in the library.
Library books are organized on library shelves according to the Dewey Decimal system. Automated systems like MARC keep track of books that are checked out. The librarian's monthly report will contain statistics, and she will not need to refer to the Dewey Decimal system to complete it. Most libraries do not have card catalogs anymore, so when a librarian helps a patron locate a specific book, she looks in her computer.

82. B: A group of interconnected computers.
Computers may be connected in a variety of ways, wired or wireless, for a variety of purposes. Answer A refers to an Internet server such as Yahoo. Answers C and D refer to software that can be used on a computer.

83. B: Students and staff can easily find books and other materials.
Since the main purpose of having a school library is to benefit students, a well-organized catalog and shelving system accomplishes that goal. Answer A, a neat library, is a nice feature of a library, but it is not as important as answer B. Answer C may not be a result of careful processing of materials, but of other factors. Answer D, a good evaluation for the librarian, may or may not happen because a number of other factors enter into an evaluation.

84. A: Acceptable Use Policy.
The Acceptable Use Policy outlines ethical computer research needs, such as plagiarism and other kinds of copyright violation. By signing it, students and parents agree to abide by its regulations. Answers B, C and D are not valid documents.

85. D: All of the above.
If the librarian knows the topic a class will be studying in advance, she will have time to set aside books on the topic at the students' reading level, plan a lesson on how best to research this particular topic, and even deliver a set of support materials to the classroom.

Copyright © Mometrix Media. You have been licensed one copy of this document for personal use only. Any other reproduction or redistribution is strictly prohibited. All rights reserved.

86. D: Announce at the next regular staff meeting that new materials have arrived, give a brief summary of what they are, and give a teachers a handout that lists all of these materials.
The librarian's report is backed up by the written materials list. Answer A, make an announcement and read aloud the titles, is not practical because it would take too long. Also, teachers might not be listening, as morning announcements are generally directed to students. Answer B does not give enough information for the teacher to decide which new materials are worth scrutinizing. Also, there is no guarantee the teachers will read the memo. Answer C, posting a list on the checkout desk, does not guarantee that very many teachers will see the list because most books are checked out by students.

87. D: Three to five years.
In a middle school, a fixed library schedule is oftentimes used to provide a prep period for teachers. A flexible schedule would eliminate library time as prep time, and the school would need to hire additional staff to cover the prep periods. School board approval might be required, depending on district regulations. If the librarian can gradually phase in the flexible scheduling, perhaps one grade level per year, her plan is more likely to be approved.

88. B: Book reviews of favorite books given by students who have read these books.
Family night is an opportunity for the librarian to celebrate what students have accomplished in the library. Student-produced materials, including book reviews, oral reports, and research-based art projects, should be part of every family gathering at the library. The other activities would probably not be very successful. If the librarian gathers young children and reads them a story, she is removing herself from the other people attending family night. If she gives a speech or if the principal gives a speech, the audience will not be as impressed with the library as they would be by seeing their own children's work on display.

89. C: The librarian informs the local television station and invites them to send a film crew. She asks that a mention of the event be made during the evening news a few days before.
Involving the local media is the most effective way to inform a whole community of a special event. Students cannot be depended on to remember an oral announcement, whether it comes over the classroom speaker or is told to a group by the librarian. Likewise, the librarian cannot be certain that flyers will be taken home.

90. B: The librarian can assist the student in finding information on the same topic from a different viewpoint. This situation provides the librarian with an opportunity to teach the student how to assess the reliability of information found on the Internet.
Answer A is not wrong, but it is not the best course of action. The librarian can tell the student that this website is biased, and not to trust it, but it is not the best solution because the student may face the same problem again. Teaching someone how to recognize biased language or to recognize that a certain website is run by an organization with a strong viewpoint will give a student much-needed analysis skills for the future. Answer C is something to be done in the future, but it will not help this student in the present. Answer D leaves all the responsibility up to the student to find more websites and compare them. The student needs established criteria before comparing information from different sources.

Copyright © Mometrix Media. You have been licensed one copy of this document for personal use only. Any other reproduction or redistribution is strictly prohibited. All rights reserved.

91. D: Enlist the help of students in creating an evaluation system so that they understand and have some ownership of it.

The best way to evaluate students is to let them know the criteria from the beginning so that they understand the librarian's expectations. If they have been involved in drawing up the criteria, they will be more accepting of the librarian's evaluation of their progress. Answer A, start each lesson with a pop quiz, would not be practical because some students might have missed the lesson. Also a quiz tests only knowledge, not performance. Answer B, point out student errors, requires the librarian to be careful not to alienate students by embarrassing them and does not foster change. Answer C, incorporate unacceptable behavior into grades, would make the grades too ambiguous. The librarian should evaluate growth in library skills. Generally, most reporting forms have a section where the evaluator can indicate a need for behavior improvement.

92. D: All of the above.

Every state has standards for student performance at each level and in each subject. The library educational program is included. If the librarian's report indicates which standards the library program has assisted students in meeting, the school principal will probably accept the need for materials to continue this success. Standards are a useful way for the librarian to check off the goals she is trying to meet through her instruction.

93. B: The arrangement of computers so that each one can be seen by the librarian.

The librarian must be able to view computer screens easily so that she can quickly help any student who needs assistance. Lighting is not generally a factor in computer placement because the screens are bright enough to be visible in most lighting situations. The age of the computer is not relevant to where in the media center it is placed. Students at computers are no more easily distracted by noise than students elsewhere in the media center.

94. C: The circulation policy controls the ease of access to materials in the media center.

A circulation policy should make the continual use of library materials possible. If the policy is too strict, patrons will have difficulty accessing some materials. For example, a checkout period of three weeks means that no one else can access that book until it is returned. A shorter period would be better. Answer A, whether or not students should pay fines, may be part of a circulation policy, but it is not the most important reason for having one. Answer B refers specifically to automated check-in and does not refer to a circulation policy. Answer D is probably true, but again, it is not the main reason for having a workable circulation policy.

95. D: Have the students leave their computers and gather around one computer so that they can observe the librarian as she models what they should do.

By modeling what students can do, the librarian can demonstrate to the whole group at the same time what the correct procedures are. If she tries to help students individually, others will continue with the problem while she is spending time with one student. Assuming that the skill is important, the librarian should not give up on students' ability to master it and end their assignment Oral directions will not work as well as an actual demonstration.

96. D: All of the above.

A Power Point presentation needs to be organized with a specific design, a plan for content delivery, and a direction toward a certain audience. The librarian can guide the student to create this kind of organization for a presentation.

Copyright © Mometrix Media. You have been licensed one copy of this document for personal use only. Any other reproduction or redistribution is strictly prohibited. All rights reserved.

97. A: A sweep means that remaining library funds will become unavailable.
Near the end of the year, the administration may "sweep" all remaining unspent funds into a surplus account. This makes them unavailable for use. The school librarian needs to have spent her funds before this happens. If she does not, a reduction in the next year's funding is also possible. If the library budget has money left over, the administration may conclude that the library is overfunded and reduce the budget for the following year. Answer C, the school expects the funds to be spent, is not relevant to a sweep. Answer D, the administration will be unhappy, is also not as important as spending the funds before that happens.

98. B: Information literacy concepts.
Information literacy includes the ability to locate necessary information through whatever methods are appropriate, whether technological or written. Students who are information literate know how to find material for a report and also know how to find a good book to read for pleasure. Answer A, the Dewey Decimal System, is not as important to students as it used to be. They can use a computer to locate a book or magazine and at the same time discover the Dewey Decimal number that tells where the material is shelved. Answer C, improving reading skills, is a task for the classroom teacher. Answer D is an activity the school librarian should provide, but it is not the most important goal of the librarian's instruction.

99. C: When the book is about an obscure subject.
All of the answers represent possible reasons for an interlibrary loan, but such loans are usually requested in a case when only one teacher or student is apt to use the book because it is about an obscure subject. In that case, the cost, the ability to buy the book, and whether it is controversial do not matter because there is no point in purchasing a book that only one or two people are likely to use.

100. B: A librarian will receive information about other libraries that she can use to improve her own program.
By keeping in touch with professional colleagues, the librarian will have an opportunity to share her ideas and accomplishments and at the same time learn new ideas from her colleagues. Answer A is incorrect because librarians from other schools, districts, or communities are not likely to step forward in support of someone in a different library. If the librarian needs advocates for a new idea, her best sources will be the parents and staff at her own school. Answer B, making friends, is incorrect because it is a side effect of networking and not the main professional benefit. Answer D is unlikely because the librarian who networks probably receives as much new information as she shares and will find that other librarians are discovering the same new technologies that she is.

Copyright © Mometrix Media. You have been licensed one copy of this document for personal use only. Any other reproduction or redistribution is strictly prohibited. All rights reserved.

Special Report: What Your Test Score Will Tell You About Your IQ

Did you know that most standardized tests correlate very strongly with IQ? In fact, your general intelligence is a better predictor of your success than any other factor, and most tests intentionally measure this trait to some degree to ensure that those selected by the test are truly qualified for the test's purposes.

Before we can delve into the relation between your test score and IQ, I will first have to explain what exactly is IQ. Here's the formula:

Your IQ = 100 + (Number of standard deviations below or above the average)*15

Now, let's define standard deviations by using an example. If we have 5 people with 5 different heights, then first we calculate the average. Let's say the average was 65 inches. The standard deviation is the "average distance" away from the average of each of the members. It is a direct measure of variability - if the 5 people included Jackie Chan and Shaquille O'Neal, obviously there's a lot more variability in that group than a group of 5 sisters who are all within 6 inches in height of each other. The standard deviation uses a number to characterize the average range of difference within a group.

A convenient feature of most groups is that they have a "normal" distribution- makes sense that most things would be normal, right? Without getting into a bunch of statistical mumbo-jumbo, you just need to know that if you know the average of the group and the standard deviation, you can successfully predict someone's percentile rank in the group.

Confused? Let me give you an example. If instead of 5 people's heights, we had 100 people, we could figure out their rank in height JUST by knowing the average, standard deviation, and their height. We wouldn't need to know each person's height and manually rank them, we could just predict their rank based on three numbers.

What this means is that you can take your PERCENTILE rank that is often given with your test and relate this to your RELATIVE IQ of people taking the test - that is, your IQ relative to the people taking the test. Obviously, there's no way to know your actual IQ because the people taking a standardized test are usually not very good samples of the general population- many of those with extremely low IQ's never achieve a level of success or competency necessary to complete a typical standardized test. In fact, professional psychologists who measure IQ actually have to use non-written tests that can fairly measure the IQ of those not able to complete a traditional test.

The bottom line is to not take your test score too seriously, but it is fun to compute your "relative IQ" among the people who took the test with you. I've done the calculations below. Just look up your percentile rank in the left and then you'll see your "relative IQ" for your test in the right hand column-

Copyright © Mometrix Media. You have been licensed one copy of this document for personal use only. Any other reproduction or redistribution is strictly prohibited. All rights reserved.

Percentile Rank	Your Relative IQ		Percentile Rank	Your Relative IQ
99	135		59	103
98	131		58	103
97	128		57	103
96	126		56	102
95	125		55	102
94	123		54	102
93	122		53	101
92	121		52	101
91	120		51	100
90	119		50	100
89	118		49	100
88	118		48	99
87	117		47	99
86	116		46	98
85	116		45	98
84	115		44	98
83	114		43	97
82	114		42	97
81	113		41	97
80	113		40	96
79	112		39	96
78	112		38	95
77	111		37	95
76	111		36	95
75	110		35	94
74	110		34	94
73	109		33	93
72	109		32	93
71	108		31	93
70	108		30	92
69	107		29	92
68	107		28	91
67	107		27	91
66	106		26	90
65	106		25	90
64	105		24	89
63	105		23	89
62	105		22	88
61	104		21	88
60	104		20	87

Copyright © Mometrix Media. You have been licensed one copy of this document for personal use only. Any other reproduction or redistribution is strictly prohibited. All rights reserved.

Special Report: What is Test Anxiety and How to Overcome It?

The very nature of tests caters to some level of anxiety, nervousness or tension, just as we feel for any important event that occurs in our lives. A little bit of anxiety or nervousness can be a good thing. It helps us with motivation, and makes achievement just that much sweeter. However, too much anxiety can be a problem; especially if it hinders our ability to function and perform.

"Test anxiety," is the term that refers to the emotional reactions that some test-takers experience when faced with a test or exam. Having a fear of testing and exams is based upon a rational fear, since the test-taker's performance can shape the course of an academic career. Nevertheless, experiencing excessive fear of examinations will only interfere with the test-takers ability to perform, and his/her chances to be successful.

There are a large variety of causes that can contribute to the development and sensation of test anxiety. These include, but are not limited to lack of performance and worrying about issues surrounding the test.

Lack of Preparation

Lack of preparation can be identified by the following behaviors or situations:

Not scheduling enough time to study, and therefore cramming the night before the test or exam
Managing time poorly, to create the sensation that there is not enough time to do everything
Failing to organize the text information in advance, so that the study material consists of the entire text and not simply the pertinent information
Poor overall studying habits

Worrying, on the other hand, can be related to both the test taker, or many other factors around him/her that will be affected by the results of the test. These include worrying about:

Previous performances on similar exams, or exams in general
How friends and other students are achieving
The negative consequences that will result from a poor grade or failure

There are three primary elements to test anxiety. Physical components, which involve the same typical bodily reactions as those to acute anxiety (to be discussed below). Emotional factors have to do with fear or panic. Mental or cognitive issues concerning attention spans and memory abilities.

Copyright © Mometrix Media. You have been licensed one copy of this document for personal use only. Any other reproduction or redistribution is strictly prohibited. All rights reserved.

Physical Signals

There are many different symptoms of test anxiety, and these are not limited to mental and emotional strain. Frequently there are a range of physical signals that will let a test taker know that he/she is suffering from test anxiety. These bodily changes can include the following:

Perspiring
Sweaty palms
Wet, trembling hands
Nausea
Dry mouth
A knot in the stomach
Headache
Faintness
Muscle tension
Aching shoulders, back and neck
Rapid heart beat
Feeling too hot/cold

To recognize the sensation of test anxiety, a test-taker should monitor him/herself for the following sensations:

The physical distress symptoms as listed above
Emotional sensitivity, expressing emotional feelings such as the need to cry or laugh too much, or a sensation of anger or helplessness
A decreased ability to think, causing the test-taker to blank out or have racing thoughts that are hard to organize or control.

Though most students will feel some level of anxiety when faced with a test or exam, the majority can cope with that anxiety and maintain it at a manageable level. However, those who cannot are faced with a very real and very serious condition, which can and should be controlled for the immeasurable benefit of this sufferer.

Naturally, these sensations lead to negative results for the testing experience. The most common effects of test anxiety have to do with nervousness and mental blocking.

Copyright © Mometrix Media. You have been licensed one copy of this document for personal use only. Any other reproduction or redistribution is strictly prohibited. All rights reserved.

Nervousness

Nervousness can appear in several different levels:

The test-taker's difficulty, or even inability to read and understand the questions on the test
The difficulty or inability to organize thoughts to a coherent form
The difficulty or inability to recall key words and concepts relating to the testing questions (especially essays)
The receipt of poor grades on a test, though the test material was well known by the test taker

Conversely, a person may also experience mental blocking, which involves:

Blanking out on test questions
Only remembering the correct answers to the questions when the test has already finished.

Fortunately for test anxiety sufferers, beating these feelings, to a large degree, has to do with proper preparation. When a test taker has a feeling of preparedness, then anxiety will be dramatically lessened.

The first step to resolving anxiety issues is to distinguish which of the two types of anxiety are being suffered. If the anxiety is a direct result of a lack of preparation, this should be considered a normal reaction, and the anxiety level (as opposed to the test results) shouldn't be anything to worry about. However, if, when adequately prepared, the test-taker still panics, blanks out, or seems to overreact, this is not a fully rational reaction. While this can be considered normal too, there are many ways to combat and overcome these effects.

Remember that anxiety cannot be entirely eliminated, however, there are ways to minimize it, to make the anxiety easier to manage. Preparation is one of the best ways to minimize test anxiety. Therefore the following techniques are wise in order to best fight off any anxiety that may want to build.

To begin with, try to avoid cramming before a test, whenever it is possible. By trying to memorize an entire term's worth of information in one day, you'll be shocking your system, and not giving yourself a very good chance to absorb the information. This is an easy path to anxiety, so for those who suffer from test anxiety, cramming should not even be considered an option.

Instead of cramming, work throughout the semester to combine all of the material which is presented throughout the semester, and work on it gradually as the course goes by, making sure to master the main concepts first, leaving minor details for a week or so before the test.

To study for the upcoming exam, be sure to pose questions that may be on the examination, to gauge the ability to answer them by integrating the ideas from your texts, notes and lectures, as well as any supplementary readings.

If it is truly impossible to cover all of the information that was covered in that particular term, concentrate on the most important portions, that can be covered very well. Learn these

Copyright © Mometrix Media. You have been licensed one copy of this document for personal use only. Any other reproduction or redistribution is strictly prohibited. All rights reserved.

concepts as best as possible, so that when the test comes, a goal can be made to use these concepts as presentations of your knowledge.

In addition to study habits, changes in attitude are critical to beating a struggle with test anxiety. In fact, an improvement of the perspective over the entire test-taking experience can actually help a test taker to enjoy studying and therefore improve the overall experience. Be certain not to overemphasize the significance of the grade - know that the result of the test is neither a reflection of self worth, nor is it a measure of intelligence; one grade will not predict a person's future success.

To improve an overall testing outlook, the following steps should be tried:

Keeping in mind that the most reasonable expectation for taking a test is to expect to try to demonstrate as much of what you know as you possibly can.
Reminding ourselves that a test is only one test; this is not the only one, and there will be others.
The thought of thinking of oneself in an irrational, all-or-nothing term should be avoided at all costs.
A reward should be designated for after the test, so there's something to look forward to. Whether it be going to a movie, going out to eat, or simply visiting friends, schedule it in advance, and do it no matter what result is expected on the exam.

Test-takers should also keep in mind that the basics are some of the most important things, even beyond anti-anxiety techniques and studying. Never neglect the basic social, emotional and biological needs, in order to try to absorb information. In order to best achieve, these three factors must be held as just as important as the studying itself.

Study Steps

Remember the following important steps for studying:

Maintain healthy nutrition and exercise habits. Continue both your recreational activities and social pass times. These both contribute to your physical and emotional well being.
Be certain to get a good amount of sleep, especially the night before the test, because when you're overtired you are not able to perform to the best of your best ability.
Keep the studying pace to a moderate level by taking breaks when they are needed, and varying the work whenever possible, to keep the mind fresh instead of getting bored.
When enough studying has been done that all the material that can be learned has been learned, and the test taker is prepared for the test, stop studying and do something relaxing such as listening to music, watching a movie, or taking a warm bubble bath.

There are also many other techniques to minimize the uneasiness or apprehension that is experienced along with test anxiety before, during, or even after the examination. In fact, there are a great deal of things that can be done to stop anxiety from interfering with lifestyle and performance. Again, remember that anxiety will not be eliminated entirely, and it shouldn't be. Otherwise that "up" feeling for exams would not exist, and most of us depend on that sensation to perform better than usual. However, this anxiety has to be at a level that is manageable.

Copyright © Mometrix Media. You have been licensed one copy of this document for personal use only.
Any other reproduction or redistribution is strictly prohibited. All rights reserved.

Of course, as we have just discussed, being prepared for the exam is half the battle right away. Attending all classes, finding out what knowledge will be expected on the exam, and knowing the exam schedules are easy steps to lowering anxiety. Keeping up with work will remove the need to cram, and efficient study habits will eliminate wasted time. Studying should be done in an ideal location for concentration, so that it is simple to become interested in the material and give it complete attention. A method such as SQ3R (Survey, Question, Read, Recite, Review) is a wonderful key to follow to make sure that the study habits are as effective as possible, especially in the case of learning from a textbook. Flashcards are great techniques for memorization. Learning to take good notes will mean that notes will be full of useful information, so that less sifting will need to be done to seek out what is pertinent for studying. Reviewing notes after class and then again on occasion will keep the information fresh in the mind. From notes that have been taken summary sheets and outlines can be made for simpler reviewing.

A study group can also be a very motivational and helpful place to study, as there will be a sharing of ideas, all of the minds can work together, to make sure that everyone understands, and the studying will be made more interesting because it will be a social occasion.

Basically, though, as long as the test-taker remains organized and self confident, with efficient study habits, less time will need to be spent studying, and higher grades will be achieved.

To become self confident, there are many useful steps. The first of these is "self talk." It has been shown through extensive research, that self-talk for students who suffer from test anxiety, should be well monitored, in order to make sure that it contributes to self confidence as opposed to sinking the student. Frequently the self talk of test-anxious students is negative or self-defeating, thinking that everyone else is smarter and faster, that they always mess up, and that if they don't do well, they'll fail the entire course. It is important to decreasing anxiety that awareness is made of self talk. Try writing any negative self thoughts and then disputing them with a positive statement instead. Begin self-encouragement as though it was a friend speaking. Repeat positive statements to help reprogram the mind to believing in successes instead of failures.

Helpful Techniques

Other extremely helpful techniques include:

Self-visualization of doing well and reaching goals
While aiming for an "A" level of understanding, don't try to "overprotect" by setting your expectations lower. This will only convince the mind to stop studying in order to meet the lower expectations.
Don't make comparisons with the results or habits of other students. These are individual factors, and different things work for different people, causing different results.
Strive to become an expert in learning what works well, and what can be done in order to improve. Consider collecting this data in a journal.
Create rewards for after studying instead of doing things before studying that will only turn into avoidance behaviors.
Make a practice of relaxing - by using methods such as progressive relaxation, self-hypnosis, guided imagery, etc - in order to make relaxation an automatic sensation.

Copyright © Mometrix Media. You have been licensed one copy of this document for personal use only. Any other reproduction or redistribution is strictly prohibited. All rights reserved.

Work on creating a state of relaxed concentration so that concentrating will take on the focus of the mind, so that none will be wasted on worrying.
Take good care of the physical self by eating well and getting enough sleep.
Plan in time for exercise and stick to this plan.

Beyond these techniques, there are other methods to be used before, during and after the test that will help the test-taker perform well in addition to overcoming anxiety.

Before the exam comes the academic preparation. This involves establishing a study schedule and beginning at least one week before the actual date of the test. By doing this, the anxiety of not having enough time to study for the test will be automatically eliminated. Moreover, this will make the studying a much more effective experience, ensuring that the learning will be an easier process. This relieves much undue pressure on the test-taker.

Summary sheets, note cards, and flash cards with the main concepts and examples of these main concepts should be prepared in advance of the actual studying time. A topic should never be eliminated from this process. By omitting a topic because it isn't expected to be on the test is only setting up the test-taker for anxiety should it actually appear on the exam. Utilize the course syllabus for laying out the topics that should be studied. Carefully go over the notes that were made in class, paying special attention to any of the issues that the professor took special care to emphasize while lecturing in class. In the textbooks, use the chapter review, or if possible, the chapter tests, to begin your review.

It may even be possible to ask the instructor what information will be covered on the exam, or what the format of the exam will be (for example, multiple choice, essay, free form, true-false). Additionally, see if it is possible to find out how many questions will be on the test. If a review sheet or sample test has been offered by the professor, make good use of it, above anything else, for the preparation for the test. Another great resource for getting to know the examination is reviewing tests from previous semesters. Use these tests to review, and aim to achieve a 100% score on each of the possible topics. With a few exceptions, the goal that you set for yourself is the highest one that you will reach.

Take all of the questions that were assigned as homework, and rework them to any other possible course material. The more problems reworked, the more skill and confidence will form as a result. When forming the solution to a problem, write out each of the steps. Don't simply do head work. By doing as many steps on paper as possible, much clarification and therefore confidence will be formed. Do this with as many homework problems as possible, before checking the answers. By checking the answer after each problem, a reinforcement will exist, that will not be on the exam. Study situations should be as exam-like as possible, to prime the test-taker's system for the experience. By waiting to check the answers at the end, a psychological advantage will be formed, to decrease the stress factor.

Another fantastic reason for not cramming is the avoidance of confusion in concepts, especially when it comes to mathematics. 8-10 hours of study will become one hundred percent more effective if it is spread out over a week or at least several days, instead of doing it all in one sitting. Recognize that the human brain requires time in order to assimilate new material, so frequent breaks and a span of study time over several days will be much more beneficial.

Copyright © Mometrix Media. You have been licensed one copy of this document for personal use only. Any other reproduction or redistribution is strictly prohibited. All rights reserved.

Additionally, don't study right up until the point of the exam. Studying should stop a minimum of one hour before the exam begins. This allows the brain to rest and put things in their proper order. This will also provide the time to become as relaxed as possible when going into the examination room. The test-taker will also have time to eat well and eat sensibly. Know that the brain needs food as much as the rest of the body. With enough food and enough sleep, as well as a relaxed attitude, the body and the mind are primed for success.

Avoid any anxious classmates who are talking about the exam. These students only spread anxiety, and are not worth sharing the anxious sentimentalities.

Before the test also involves creating a positive attitude, so mental preparation should also be a point of concentration. There are many keys to creating a positive attitude. Should fears become rushing in, make a visualization of taking the exam, doing well, and seeing an A written on the paper. Write out a list of affirmations that will bring a feeling of confidence, such as "I am doing well in my English class," "I studied well and know my material," "I enjoy this class." Even if the affirmations aren't believed at first, it sends a positive message to the subconscious which will result in an alteration of the overall belief system, which is the system that creates reality.

If a sensation of panic begins, work with the fear and imagine the very worst! Work through the entire scenario of not passing the test, failing the entire course, and dropping out of school, followed by not getting a job, and pushing a shopping cart through the dark alley where you'll live. This will place things into perspective! Then, practice deep breathing and create a visualization of the opposite situation - achieving an "A" on the exam, passing the entire course, receiving the degree at a graduation ceremony.

On the day of the test, there are many things to be done to ensure the best results, as well as the most calm outlook. The following stages are suggested in order to maximize test-taking potential:

Begin the examination day with a moderate breakfast, and avoid any coffee or beverages with caffeine if the test taker is prone to jitters. Even people who are used to managing caffeine can feel jittery or light-headed when it is taken on a test day.
Attempt to do something that is relaxing before the examination begins. As last minute cramming clouds the mastering of overall concepts, it is better to use this time to create a calming outlook.
Be certain to arrive at the test location well in advance, in order to provide time to select a location that is away from doors, windows and other distractions, as well as giving enough time to relax before the test begins.
Keep away from anxiety generating classmates who will upset the sensation of stability and relaxation that is being attempted before the exam.
Should the waiting period before the exam begins cause anxiety, create a self-distraction by reading a light magazine or something else that is relaxing and simple.

During the exam itself, read the entire exam from beginning to end, and find out how much time should be allotted to each individual problem. Once writing the exam, should more time be taken for a problem, it should be abandoned, in order to begin another problem. If there is time at the end, the unfinished problem can always be returned to and completed.

Copyright © Mometrix Media. You have been licensed one copy of this document for personal use only. Any other reproduction or redistribution is strictly prohibited. All rights reserved.

Read the instructions very carefully - twice - so that unpleasant surprises won't follow during or after the exam has ended.

When writing the exam, pretend that the situation is actually simply the completion of homework within a library, or at home. This will assist in forming a relaxed atmosphere, and will allow the brain extra focus for the complex thinking function.

Begin the exam with all of the questions with which the most confidence is felt. This will build the confidence level regarding the entire exam and will begin a quality momentum. This will also create encouragement for trying the problems where uncertainty resides.

Going with the "gut instinct" is always the way to go when solving a problem. Second guessing should be avoided at all costs. Have confidence in the ability to do well.

For essay questions, create an outline in advance that will keep the mind organized and make certain that all of the points are remembered. For multiple choice, read every answer, even if the correct one has been spotted - a better one may exist.

Continue at a pace that is reasonable and not rushed, in order to be able to work carefully. Provide enough time to go over the answers at the end, to check for small errors that can be corrected.

Should a feeling of panic begin, breathe deeply, and think of the feeling of the body releasing sand through its pores. Visualize a calm, peaceful place, and include all of the sights, sounds and sensations of this image. Continue the deep breathing, and take a few minutes to continue this with closed eyes. When all is well again, return to the test.

If a "blanking" occurs for a certain question, skip it and move on to the next question. There will be time to return to the other question later. Get everything done that can be done, first, to guarantee all the grades that can be compiled, and to build all of the confidence possible. Then return to the weaker questions to build the marks from there.

Remember, one's own reality can be created, so as long as the belief is there, success will follow. And remember: anxiety can happen later, right now, there's an exam to be written!

After the examination is complete, whether there is a feeling for a good grade or a bad grade, don't dwell on the exam, and be certain to follow through on the reward that was promised...and enjoy it! Don't dwell on any mistakes that have been made, as there is nothing that can be done at this point anyway.

Additionally, don't begin to study for the next test right away. Do something relaxing for a while, and let the mind relax and prepare itself to begin absorbing information again.

From the results of the exam - both the grade and the entire experience, be certain to learn from what has gone on. Perfect studying habits and work some more on confidence in order to make the next examination experience even better than the last one.

Learn to avoid places where openings occurred for laziness, procrastination and day dreaming.

Copyright © Mometrix Media. You have been licensed one copy of this document for personal use only. Any other reproduction or redistribution is strictly prohibited. All rights reserved.

Use the time between this exam and the next one to better learn to relax, even learning to relax on cue, so that any anxiety can be controlled during the next exam. Learn how to relax the body. Slouch in your chair if that helps. Tighten and then relax all of the different muscle groups, one group at a time, beginning with the feet and then working all the way up to the neck and face. This will ultimately relax the muscles more than they were to begin with. Learn how to breathe deeply and comfortably, and focus on this breathing going in and out as a relaxing thought. With every exhale, repeat the word "relax."

As common as test anxiety is, it is very possible to overcome it. Make yourself one of the test-takers who overcome this frustrating hindrance.

Copyright © Mometrix Media. You have been licensed one copy of this document for personal use only. Any other reproduction or redistribution is strictly prohibited. All rights reserved.

Special Report: Retaking the Test: What Are Your Chances at Improving Your Score?

After going through the experience of taking a major test, many test takers feel that once is enough. The test usually comes during a period of transition in the test taker's life, and taking the test is only one of a series of important events. With so many distractions and conflicting recommendations, it may be difficult for a test taker to rationally determine whether or not he should retake the test after viewing his scores.

The importance of the test usually only adds to the burden of the retake decision. However, don't be swayed by emotion. There a few simple questions that you can ask yourself to guide you as you try to determine whether a retake would improve your score:

1. What went wrong? Why wasn't your score what you expected?

Can you point to a single factor or problem that you feel caused the low score? Were you sick on test day? Was there an emotional upheaval in your life that caused a distraction? Were you late for the test or not able to use the full time allotment? If you can point to any of these specific, individual problems, then a retake should definitely be considered.

2. Is there enough time to improve?

Many problems that may show up in your score report may take a lot of time for improvement. A deficiency in a particular math skill may require weeks or months of tutoring and studying to improve. If you have enough time to improve an identified weakness, then a retake should definitely be considered.

3. How will additional scores be used? Will a score average, highest score, or most recent score be used?

Different test scores may be handled completely differently. If you've taken the test multiple times, sometimes your highest score is used, sometimes your average score is computed and used, and sometimes your most recent score is used. Make sure you understand what method will be used to evaluate your scores, and use that to help you determine whether a retake should be considered.

4. Are my practice test scores significantly higher than my actual test score?

If you have taken a lot of practice tests and are consistently scoring at a much higher level than your actual test score, then you should consider a retake. However, if you've taken five practice tests and only one of your scores was higher than your actual test score, or if your practice test scores were only slightly higher than your actual test score, then it is unlikely that you will significantly increase your score.

5. Do I need perfect scores or will I be able to live with this score? Will this score still allow me to follow my dreams?

Copyright © Mometrix Media. You have been licensed one copy of this document for personal use only. Any other reproduction or redistribution is strictly prohibited. All rights reserved.

What kind of score is acceptable to you? Is your current score "good enough?" Do you have to have a certain score in order to pursue the future of your dreams? If you won't be happy with your current score, and there's no way that you could live with it, then you should consider a retake. However, don't get your hopes up. If you are looking for significant improvement, that may or may not be possible. But if you won't be happy otherwise, it is at least worth the effort. Remember that there are other considerations. To achieve your dream, it is likely that your grades may also be taken into account. A great test score is usually not the only thing necessary to succeed. Make sure that you aren't overemphasizing the importance of a high test score.

Furthermore, a retake does not always result in a higher score. Some test takers will score lower on a retake, rather than higher. One study shows that one-fourth of test takers will achieve a significant improvement in test score, while one-sixth of test takers will actually show a decrease. While this shows that most test takers will improve, the majority will only improve their scores a little and a retake may not be worth the test taker's effort.

Finally, if a test is taken only once and is considered in the added context of good grades on the part of a test taker, the person reviewing the grades and scores may be tempted to assume that the test taker just had a bad day while taking the test, and may discount the low test score in favor of the high grades. But if the test is retaken and the scores are approximately the same, then the validity of the low scores are only confirmed. Therefore, a retake could actually hurt a test taker by definitely bracketing a test taker's score ability to a limited range.

Copyright © Mometrix Media. You have been licensed one copy of this document for personal use only. Any other reproduction or redistribution is strictly prohibited. All rights reserved.